The Beginning of the End

The End Times from a Middle Eastern Perspective

Jerry Mattix

To the children of my children -

All the ends of the earth shall remember and turn to the LORD,
and all the families of the nations shall worship before you. For
kingship belongs to the LORD, and he rules over the nations. All the
prosperous of the earth eat and worship; before him shall bow all
who go down to the dust, even the one who could not keep himself
alive. Posterity shall serve him; it shall be told of the Lord to the
coming generation; they shall come and proclaim his righteousness
to a people yet unborn, that he has done it (Psalm 22:27-31).

CONTENTS

FOREWORD

This book is for anyone interested in the future, which should be all of us. In these pages, Jerry Mattix distills years of experience teaching on the subject of the Last Days into one book.

Jerry's exceptional teaching gift is at its best here. Do you have trouble making sense of eschatology in general and the Book of Revelation in particular? Struggling with the signs of the times? Are you confused by the order of the Last Days events described in both the Old and New Testaments? Here is a clear and accessible explanation of the subject of the Last Days.

Theology is progressive. That is, God reveals truth over time. The Book of Revelation, a manual for how Christians can be overcomers during times of persecution, makes even more sense in the 21st century than it did when it was recorded in the 1st century. Jerry shares unique insights from John's revelation that would have been inconceivable to first century Christians but which come clearly into focus in our day, especially in today's Middle East. And this is Jerry's unique contribution to the subject; he is a veteran resident and cogent observer of this volatile area of the world and also an insightful commentator of the Scriptures.

Born and raised in Bolivia, the son of missionaries, he graduated from Bible College in the United States and then followed God's call to Turkey. Jerry and his wife, Sarah, also the daughter of missionaries to Mexico and later Spain, made a home and raised three children in the city of Diyarbakir in southeastern Turkey. In addition to pastoring, he developed a Turkish-language discipleship training program for Muslim background believers. While teaching on the subject of eschatology, Jerry started to connect the dots concerning what

John was seeing and describing in the Revelation, back in the 1st century, to modern day events in the Middle East, particularly in Turkey.

When Jerry was expelled from Turkey, after twelve years of ministry in Diyarbakir, he relocated his family to North Cyprus. In 2014, he founded the Middle East School of Disciples - MESD. He translated the curriculum he wrote and taught in Turkish to English and invited Muslim background believers with proficiency in English to attend the two-week long intensive. The MESD is a survey course that covers all sixty-six books of the Bible in addition to lectures on topical subjects. I met Jerry in Diyarbakir in 2004 and guest-taught in his discipleship program in Diyarbakir. We've enjoyed a happy and memorable collaboration since, even as he invited me to be a lecturer at the inaugural MESD and every year since.

Luther had an aversion to the Book of Revelation, Zwingli rejected it from the canon of Scripture, and Calvin never wrote a commentary on it. Yet, year after year, I have found Jerry's closing MESD lecture on Revelation to be a particular favorite of mine. The reason is because the scenes described by the apostle John, which previous generations of Christians found fantastic and bizarre, are actually conceivable and understandable in our day. Jerry's treatment of the subject of the Last Days takes into consideration the dizzying pace of change in every sphere of modern day life, whether socially, economically, politically, or militarily, which makes his insights that much more relevant and applicable.

Jesus' first coming inaugurated the beginning of the Last Days. Why is this important? Keeping the end goal in mind and in sight affects everything we do every day of our lives until His glorious return or until we are resurrected from the dead to everlasting life.

We are at a time of unprecedented change accelerated by social media; we also live in uncertain times. Jerry helps us make sense of the Last Days and in doing so, prepares us for today and for the future. We are people of hope and Jerry's book is a narrative of hope based on rigorous and integrated biblical exegesis.

The best is yet to come.

Robert Sakr
Beirut, Lebanon

PROLOGUE

I learned my eschatology from my Dad. He and Mom have been serving the Lord as missionaries in Bolivia for over 50 years. Both of them have been a great inspiration to me and I owe much of my love for God's work and the Bible to them. Consequently, the following words from my Dad, Mark Mattix mean a whole lot to me:

I am a great admirer of Sir Robert Anderson and hold great respect for John Nelson Darby. Dispensational theology appeared to be the key for putting the puzzle of eschatology together. I thought that Dwight Pentecost was the last word on the subject. But he is not. Scripture is the last word.

So, I am thankful that Jerry has forced me to reconsider the subject. He points out places where the pieces don't fit together so neatly and where we carry over certain suppositions from the time of the reformation (i. e. the identity of the fourth beast).

Jerry's Middle East perspective may shed light on how everything is coming together. The world's balance of power has altered considerably since J. N. Darby sat down to solve this puzzle 200 years ago. Above all, I want to let God's Word speak for itself. Like prophets before us and angels above, we should "search intently and with the greatest care, trying to find out the time and circumstances which the Spirit of Christ predicted the glories that would follow Christ's sufferings" (1 Peter 1:11).

INTRODUCTION

Bringing up the end times is sure to animate any conversation. In fact, divergent eschatological interpretations have been known to separate the best of friends and divide whole communities. Moreover, down through history certain end times' scenarios have even been perceived as existential threats by some nations.

In 2011 I wrote an article regarding the potential role the modern Republic of Turkey might play in the Biblical end times framework. At the time I shared it with a number of pastors in the region who largely agreed with my analysis but urged me not to publish my views due to the volatile nature of the Turkish authorities. However, even though I acquiesced to their recommendations and chose to write a more general book on eschatology in Turkish, a year later I was banned from entering Turkey where I had lived with my family and ministered in the local churches for over a decade. I was told that I was deemed a "threat to national security."

I promptly got a lawyer and pursued every legal means to clear my name and reenter Turkey. After three years, I finally succeeded in winning my case, however, in the process my lawyer received a list of bogus accusations made against me which included fomenting political insurrection and clandestine missionary work. However, among the supporting evidences for the accusations leveled against me, one in particular caught my attention. They listed my unpublished article about the end times. Not only does this mean that the

Republic of Turkey was reading my private correspondence but also that my mention of Turkey as a potential candidate for the end times' beast registered on their radar, enough for them to brand me a threat to national security.

Needless to say, since our expulsion from Turkey my family and I have found other means to continue serving God and sharing the gospel of Jesus Christ in the Middle East. In the years since then, I've continued to keep my eye on the signs of the times even as I dig deeper into the relevant Scriptures all of which has served to hone my eschatological perspective even further. I have also noted that my premonition that the nations of the Middle East and Islam in particular might play an instrumental role in the end times scenario is increasingly being championed by others across the Christian landscape. Moreover, I'm convinced more than ever that in seeking to understand the fulfillment of the myriads of prophetic passages in Scriptures we need to approach the Bible from a Middle Eastern perspective.

One of the foundational axioms of Biblical eschatology that we must keep in mind as we seek to match the prophetic text with world events, is the fact that the Bible presents prophecy from a Middle Eastern vantage point. Consequently, in our analysis of current events, we must look specifically for those matters that relate to Israel in particular and the Middle East in general. To put it bluntly Biblical prophecy is not so concerned with western interests as it is with how events directly affect God's plan for His people. In short, Israel is the context of the Bible. In fact, the Jewish nation has always been the lens through which the Bible looks at events both in the past and in the future, so we would do well to look through the same periscope.

In the chapters that follow I will not delve into all the topics related to eschatology, as they are too many to address in one book, and they require more expertise than I possess. Rather, my aim is to touch on certain key end times' subjects that I believe are better understood from a Middle Eastern perspective. This in particular as it relates to the end times' beast prophesied both by Daniel and the apostle John in the Revelation. I would also like to draw attention to another way of viewing the rapture, which attempts to incorporate the critical elements of opposing perspectives on this hotly debated issue. Throughout my book, I promote a 'both/and' approach to eschatology rather than the usual 'either/or' status quo. Finally, I will present an exegetical summary of the book of Revelation which strives to do justice to its Biblical context while allowing the natural development of the text to speak for itself.

I do not claim to be a prophet or to have put the eschatological puzzle together all the way. On the contrary, studying for this book has challenged me to revisit and even change my position on some matters, and I'm sure it won't be the last time. Still, I do believe my years of ministering and studying God's Word in the Middle East have helped to clarify many key issues for me. My hope and prayer is that these observations will also help my readers to gain a greater appreciation and enthusiasm for God's global plan of redemption culminating in the glorious return and kingdom of our Lord Jesus Christ. Indeed it weighs heavily on me that the church must urgently recover its love for the appearing of Christ even as we see the day fast approaching. *"For salvation is nearer to us now than when we first believed. The night is far gone; the day is at hand"* (Romans 13:11-12a).

1. THE IMPERATIVE

Some may be asking, why we even bother to try to sort out the end times. God has it all under control, right? What business do we have trying to make sense of things yet future; let's just focus on making our world a better place... These objections largely undergird the lackadaisical attitude displayed by many people towards the subject of the end times. In some people, we can sense open contempt and even hostility towards this subject. This is largely due to the periodic appearances of false prophets who make a mockery of Biblical prophecy even as they ignore the clear warnings of Christ with regards to the timing of his return. Of course we are not surprised by these developments as the Scriptures clearly warn us of such abuses and their consequent reactions. These tragic incidents far from diminishing the great importance of the subject at hand, only serve to underscore its enormous significance.

Before delving into eschatological minutia I want to take time to lay the groundwork for why I believe it is imperative that we study this subject. Much like a wild but majestic stallion that resists all attempts to be tamed, Biblical eschatology has suffered much at the hands of both its proponents and opponents. Our inability to master this great subject does not in any way depreciate its value, rather it only accentuates it. But it also reminds us that we must approach the task at hand with great humility and tremendous respect for the Biblical text. If you are already convinced of the importance of this matter then feel free to move on to the next chapter.

First let me clarify what we mean by the "Last Days" or "End Times." This term is used in the Bible to refer to the culmination of God's purposes in human history. The Old Testament prophets often spoke of this yet future time in great detail (Isaiah 2:2; Ezekiel 38:16; Daniel 10:14). After the first advent of Christ, the New Testament writers seemed to view themselves as living in at least the beginning of the latter days (Acts 2:17; Hebrews 1:2; 1 John 2:18). They also looked forward with great anticipation to the consummation of God's purposes on earth and spoke at length about the signs of the end times (2 Thessalonians 2:1-12; 2 Timothy 3:1-3; 2 Peter 3:3-13).

The Bible is full of references to the end of human history. In fact some scholars have calculated that up to 30% of the Scriptures, at the time they were written, were prophetic or futuristic in nature.[1] Many of these ancient predictions were fulfilled in the New Testament. It is estimated that roughly 300 prophecies regarding the life and work of Jesus Christ were fulfilled in his first coming, and these with remarkable accuracy. However, there remain roughly 2,300 prophecies yet to be fulfilled with regard to his second coming.[2] This alone suffices to highlight the quintessential place that prophecy plays in the unfolding of the Biblical drama.

God's Fingerprints

One of the main reasons the prophetic seems to feature so prominently in the Scriptures is because it serves as a litmus test of the Bible's authenticity and God's authority. From ancient times there has always been a great fascination with knowing the future. This was the shady business of soothsayers, oracles and astrologers who claimed to possess special knowledge of future events. In the Bible however, the one true God claims to have exclusive rights to this phenomena even as he reveals yet future events in great detail through his chosen prophets. How do we know this? In the Scriptures God actually challenges the pagan practitioners of that time to a prophetic contest.

- Isaiah 41:21-23 - *Set forth your case, says the LORD; bring your proofs, says the King of Jacob. Let them bring them, and tell us what is to happen. Tell us the former things, what they are, that we may consider them, that we may know their outcome; or **declare to us the things to come**. Tell us what is to come hereafter, that we may know that you are gods; do good, or do harm, that we may be dismayed and terrified.*

- Isaiah 44:6-7 - *Thus says the LORD, the King of Israel and his Redeemer, the LORD of hosts: "I am the first and I am the last; besides me there is no god. Who is like me? Let him proclaim it. Let him declare and set it before me, since I appointed an ancient people. **Let them declare what is to come, and what will happen.***

- Isaiah 46:9-10 - *Remember the former things of old; for I am God, and there is no other; I am God, and there is none like me, **declaring the end from the beginning** and from ancient times things not yet done, saying, 'My counsel shall stand, and I will accomplish all my purpose.'*

In this way God calls out the pagan gods and their worshippers of Isaiah's time. His challenge is based on the presupposition that one of the great tests of divinity is the ability to predict the future. Clearly none but God can know the future. Down through the centuries many a false prophet or sorcerer has tried to make people believe in their lies by pretending to have a corner on the truth but the fact remains that no other book in human history has dared to speak so boldly about the future as the Bible. Furthermore the prophecies enshrined in Scriptures are not just Nostradamus style guesswork, rather they are as precise and detailed even as their fulfillment is highly unlikely by normal processes.

In the middle of the chapters listed above, Isaiah records for us one of the most outstanding prophecies ever written.

At that time, roughly 700 B.C., the northern kingdom of Israel had been overrun by the Assyrian Empire and these were threatening to obliterate the southern kingdom of Judah as well. In the face of such a terrible onslaught Isaiah was predicting the rise of the Babylonian Empire which would one day overthrow Assyria. He predicted that the Babylonian king Nebuchadnezzar would also attack the city of Jerusalem, destroy the temple and take the Jewish people as exiles to Babylon. Everything he described actually took place around 100 years later. However Isaiah went even further when he spoke of a yet future king of the Medes and Persians named Cyrus who would defeat the Babylonians and subsequently release the people of Israel encouraging them to return to their homeland to rebuild their temple.

> Who says of Cyrus, 'He is my shepherd, and he shall fulfill all my purpose'; saying of Jerusalem, 'She shall be built,' and of the temple, 'Your foundation shall be laid. Thus says the LORD to his anointed, to Cyrus, whose right hand I have grasped, to subdue nations before him and to loose the belts of kings, to open doors before him that gates may not be closed (Isaiah 44:28-45:1).

Now if Isaiah's clear predictions of the next two successive world empires is not remarkable enough, the fact that at the time he wrote this prophecy the kingdom of Medo-Persia did not even register on the political map of the ancient world is truly amazing. What is more, writing more than 150 years before the overthrow of Babylon, Isaiah goes so far as to record the name of Cyrus the Great (twice!), who did indeed release the Jewish people encouraging them to return and rebuild the temple in Jerusalem (Ezra 1). In fact Cyrus' historic edict in which he allowed the exiled peoples conquered by his Babylonian predecessor to go back to their homelands is inscribed in the famous Cyrus cylinder which resides in the British Museum.

In this way throughout the Scriptures, the incredible level of accuracy and precision displayed in the prophecies of the Bible serves as living testimony to the fact that this is indeed God's Book. Through prophecy God has left his unique fingerprints all over the Bible, providing positive proof for his unique revelation. No other religious book dares to record prophetic predictions of this caliber lest they be exposed as fraudulent. God's Word however is replete with examples of fulfilled prophecy; consequently as the apostle Peter noted, *"we have the prophetic word more fully confirmed, to which you will do well to pay attention as to a lamp shining in a dark place, until the day dawns and the morning star rises in your hearts"* (2 Peter 1:19).

Essential To Faith

Back to our question: If God has everything under wraps why do we need to be in the know? As we noted above God takes prophecy very seriously as it provides us with indisputable evidence of divine revelation and his faithfulness to uphold his word. Furthermore, the Bible's emphasis on future events is also a vindication of God's eternal plans and ultimately his character. The world as we know it today is in terrible disarray, such that many shake their fist at heaven believing God is somehow responsible for the evil therein. God's Word sets the record straight by explaining the fall and ultimate corruption of mankind because of their own rebellion. However it then presents the redemption of mankind through Christ and ultimately the restoration of creation to God's original purposes. Not only did God not abandon mankind he brings history full circle to restoration in Christ (Ephesians 1:9-10).

In theological studies, it is often common to view eschatology, fraught as it is with controversy, almost as an elective and not a core subject. We tend to imagine it as the caboose or tag-along in the mighty train of Christian doctrine. However, the Scriptures seem to indicate quite the opposite, namely that our understanding of things future sets the course for the rest of our theology. In this regard our eschatology is much more like the locomotive of our theology powering us forward and setting the pace for our faith.

The Christian faith is a forward looking faith. Even while it teaches us to cherish God's good earth and strive for mankind's welfare, it ultimately directs our attention to a new heaven and a new earth. Thus we are encouraged not to 'lay up treasures on earth' but rather to 'set our minds on things above.' Likewise we are not to seek any earthly dominion on our own terms but rather to 'seek first the kingdom of God.' This is why our theology is replete with concepts like, redemption, regeneration and restoration.

Throughout the Old Testament we are regularly encouraged to look to the future restoration of all things, when God finally sets the record straight and righteousness reigns supreme (Isaiah 11; Daniel 12; Joel 2-3; Zechariah 14). The message of Jesus is no different, always pointing his followers towards the ultimate consummation of history (Matthew 24-25; Luke 17:22-37). The message of the apostles continued in the same vein. Even as they preached the forgiveness of sins through faith in Jesus Christ, they kept directing people to the promised restoration of all things (Acts 3:18-20, 17:30-31). The epistles echo the same eschatological theme stressing the integral part our faith in God's promises regarding the future plays in the gospel message.

> For the grace of God has appeared, bringing salvation for all people, training us to renounce ungodliness and worldly passions, and to live self-controlled, upright, and godly lives in the present age, **waiting for our blessed hope, the appearing of the glory of our great God and Savior Jesus Christ**, who gave himself for us to redeem us from all lawlessness and to purify for himself a people for his own possession who are zealous for good works (Titus 2:11-14).

The above summary of the gospel from Paul's pen stresses the central nature of Christian eschatology. We are not just saved *from* sin and hell, we are saved *for* a blessed future with our Savior. The apostles consistently stress that along with Christ's death, burial and resurrection, his second coming plays a critical role in bringing God's purposes full circle.

As Jesus prepared to leave his disciples he regularly pointed them to his second coming, reminding them that his purposes were not yet completed (Matthew 25:31; John 14:1-3). After his resurrection when he was lifted up into the clouds the apostles again received confirmation that he would return in the same way as they saw him depart (Acts 1:11). Thus we should not be surprised to see Christ's disciples described as those who 'eagerly await his appearing' (1 Corinthians 1:7; 1 Thessalonians 1:9-10; Hebrews 9:28).

From a Biblical perspective our current situation here on earth is one in which we are waiting and longing for our true and eternal home. This 'interim' is often described as 'the present age'. Regarding this 'present' condition we are warned not to fall in love with the world as it is temporal state (1 Corinthians 7:31; 2 Timothy 4:10; 1 John 2:15-17). In fact Paul further characterizes the 'present age' as evil and governed by the powers of darkness (Galatians 1:4; Ephesians 6:12). In this present age, the world is not in submission to Christ, that is why we eagerly await his return and the restoration of his kingdom (Hebrews 2:8).

The apostle Paul would seem to go even further when he stresses that without a clear understanding of things future, any faith in God is ultimately void and empty. To those that questioned the doctrine of resurrection from the dead Paul reminds them that our future is contingent on Christ's glorious resurrection which is an established fact. Thus to deny the truth of resurrection is to render the very essence of our faith vain and worthless (1 Corinthians 15:12-19). He then goes on to elaborate in great detail the order of eschatological events culminating in the consummation of history when the Son entrusts all things into the Father's hands (15:20-28). Then, in response to the question of how the dead are raised, he presents some vivid illustrations that stress the incorruptible nature of our future bodies. Finally, he unveils a divine secret, namely that those who are alive at Christ's second coming will cheat death and be instantaneously transformed and transported to glory along with all the other resurrected saints (15:50-53). Clearly a robust eschatology played a critical part in Paul's theology.

Know And Understand

Because of the controversial nature and sometimes confusing details of eschatology, many are tempted to adopt a neutral stance and not take any hard position regarding the end times. 'Who are we to say what will happen in the future...' they rationalize. Sadly, in our day and age to portray certainty or confidence in anything but human choice and equality is deemed arrogant and bigoted. And yet God's Word is chock full of definitive statements regarding future events, resurrection and judgment, heaven and hell, to name only a few. Even a cursory survey of Scriptures highlights a host of commands related to our understanding of future events. God clearly wants us to be in the know:

- Deuteronomy 29:29 - *The secret things belong to the LORD our God, but the things that are revealed belong to us and to our children forever, that we may do all the words of this law*
- Isaiah 43:19 - *Behold, I am doing a new thing; now it springs forth, do you not perceive it? I will make a way in the wilderness and rivers in the desert.*
- Hosea 14:9 - *Whoever is wise, let him understand these things; whoever is discerning, let him know them; for the ways of the LORD are right, and the upright walk in them, but transgressors stumble in them.*

- 1 Corinthians 6:2 - *Or do you not know that the saints will judge the world? And if the world is to be judged by you, are you incompetent to try trivial cases?*
- 2 Corinthians 5:1 - *For we know that if the tent that is our earthly home is destroyed, we have a building from God, a house not made with hands, eternal in the heavens.*
- 1 John 3:2 - *Beloved, we are God's children now, and what we will be has not yet appeared; but we know that when he appears we shall be like him, because we shall see him as he is.*
- 1 John 5:13 - *I write these things to you who believe in the name of the Son of God, that you may know that you have eternal life.*

For us as Christians, to express with certainty the truths revealed to us by God in his Word is by no means a sign of intellectual bigotry or spiritual snobbishness, rather it is indicative of the objective truth of our faith. To believe in something is to vouch for its reliability and authority. What could be more reliable than God's Word? Consequently, if the Scriptures give us every reason to believe in God's promises about eternal life, we would be bigoted to disagree with him. The same is true with regard to the many other passages that relate to yet future events in human history.

In his discussion of the cataclysmic events surrounding the destruction of the temple in Jerusalem and the signs of his second coming, Jesus Christ makes reference to the 'abomination of desolation' referred to in the book of Daniel (Matthew 24:15). Then he adds a striking side-comment: *"Let the reader understand."* Although short and simple it is a stark reminder that we are charged with reading and understanding the prophecies made in God's Word. It also implies that by studying these ancient texts we will indeed attain understanding of God's eternal plans and purposes.

When we turn to the relevant passage in Daniel it starts with a similarly striking phrase, *"Know therefore and understand that from the going out of the word...*" (Daniel 9:2 The command given by the angel Gabriel to the prophet is quite forthright, namely that Daniel is charged not just with recording future events but also ascertaining their meaning. Later in the same book, Daniel is overwhelmed by the prophecies entrusted to him recognizing his limitations in comprehending the message delivered. To this the divine messenger responds as follows:

> *Go your way, Daniel, for the words are shut up and sealed until the time of the end. Many shall purify themselves and make themselves white and be refined, but the wicked shall act wickedly. And none of the wicked shall understand, but those who are wise shall understand* (Daniel 12:9-10).

From Daniel's vantage point six centuries before the first advent of Christ, making any sense of the great tribulation predicted was next to impossible. However the angel does promise that as the end times draw near "*those who are wise will understand.*" What an exciting promise! In an earlier verse he also added this cryptic statement: "*Many shall run to and fro, and knowledge shall increase*" (Daniel 12:4). More than two millennia later, with the aid of the New Testament revelation, we clearly have more information than Daniel had to go on. Furthermore as the time draws nigh the picture will surely become clearer and clearer. This makes Jesus' reminder to read and understand all the more pertinent.

In this vein there is a remarkable aspect of Biblical prophecy worth mentioning. Namely, even though we have literally thousands of verses detailing events yet future recorded in the Scriptures, the eschatological picture is largely unintelligible to unbelievers and even many believers. This is because only those who eagerly study them with wisdom granted by the Holy Spirit can begin to unlock the secrets of prophecy. It is as if God has camouflaged his plans and hidden them in plain sight. However his promise remains, that as the ear those who are wise shall understand: *"In the* u *will understand this"* (Jeremiah 30:24).

count of this Jesus is heard repeatedly chiding his discip. be alert and prayerful with regard to the end times (Luke 12:37-38, 21:34-36). He further directs their attention to the parable of the fig tree:

> From the fig tree learn its lesson: as soon as its branch becomes
> tender and puts out its leaves, you know that summer is near.
> So also, when you see all these things, you know that he is near,
> at the very gates (Matthew 24:32-33).

In the following chapter of Matthew, the Lord Jesus gives two more parables about being alert and awake with reference to his second coming. Clearly this is an important subject to our Lord and the signs he has provided his disciples are evidently sufficient for them to be able to recognize future developments. In short, this is not a subject God would have us take a passive stance on, rather he expects us to be knowledgable, expectant and vigilant.

Down To Earth

The topic of eschatology is often characterized as highly speculative and out of touch with reality. While modern discussions on the subject may often turn into such, the Biblical perspective on the end times is actually quite down to earth. For the apostles and the prophets, God's future promises were by no means 'pie in the sky bye and bye.' Rather the truths of Scriptures had direct bearing on their choices in the real world.

Throughout Scriptures we come across many occasions where the authors turn to the end times as a source of encouragement in daily struggles or motivation for the task at hand (2 Thessalonians 1:6-10). As noted earlier Jesus urged his disciples to regard the immanency of his second coming as an ever-present reminder to remain faithful in service (Matthew

24:44-47). Likewise the apostle Paul draws from his teaching on the end times to encourage believers to remain strong in the spiritual battle of our day (1 Thessalonians 5:1-11). The apostle John further notes that it is our hope of being in the presence of Christ at any moment that should serve as the chief motivation for keeping ourselves pure from fleshly defilement (1 John 3:2-3). Even in the book of Revelation, where we are tempted to get caught up in eschatological visions, the apostle is careful to bring us back to earth and highlight the practical significance of his message (Revelation 16:15).

Naturally the promise of Christ's return serves as a source of strength and comfort in difficult times. But even in these instances the blessed hope is not presented as an escape mechanism or cop out from reality. Rather, the coming of the Lord is an encouragement to hold the faith and persevere in service (James 5:7-8; Jude 20-21). If anything a proper appreciation of the imminent end of all things brings a healthy sobriety to our daily life. Instead of giving way to fatalism a Biblical appreciation of the last days should spur us to more fervent prayers and radical love (1 Peter 4:7-8).

More than anything a realistic appraisal of the end of the world should truly alter our world-view and help to shape our daily priorities.

> But the day of the Lord will come like a thief, and then the heavens will pass away with a roar, and the heavenly bodies will be burned up and dissolved, and the earth and the works that are done on it will be exposed. Since all these things are thus to be dissolved, **what sort of people ought you to be** in lives of holiness and godliness, waiting for and hastening the coming of the day of God, because of which the heavens will be set on fire and dissolved, and the heavenly bodies will melt as they burn! But according to his promise we are waiting for new heavens and a new earth in which righteousness dwells. Therefore, beloved, since you are waiting for these, be diligent to be found by him without spot or blemish, and at

~uce (2 Peter 3:10-14).

Clearly the pragmatic ramifications of the end times are not lost on the apostle Peter. In fact his reflection on the unavoidable end of history elicits the all important question: 'What sort of people ought you to be?' In light of this, the ultimate reality, not only our daily choices and priorities but our whole perspective on life should be altered dramatically.

In teaching his disciples Jesus regularly put mundane matters in the greater context of the end times. He starts his great sermon on the mount by stating that the blessed are those who have attained an eternal perspective with regard to every aspect of their otherwise worldly life (Matthew 5:1-12). Later, when speaking of anger or lust he is quick remind them of the eternal ramifications of these sins (Matthew 5:22, 29). When speaking of material wealth he is quick remind his followers of its temporal nature, thus he urges them to store up treasure in heaven instead (Matthew 6:19-20). When urging his disciples not to judge one another he reminds them of the final judgment (Matthew 7:1-2). Finally he stresses that those who will ultimately attain the joys of heaven are not the pious ones but rather those who through faith in him have come to know him personally (Matthew 7:21-23).

A Biblical eschatology should not only alter our world-view and perspective of life it should in fact reshape our identity. In light of God's final judgment the apostle Peter urges believers to "*conduct yourselves with fear throughout the time of your exile*" (1 Peter 1:17). He goes further saying, "*I urge you as sojourners and exiles to abstain from the passions of the flesh, which wage war against your soul*" (1 Peter 2:11). The early Christians knew what it was like to be ostracized and exiled for their faith. However instead of resenting this they embraced this new identity recognizing that their true home was with the Lord in heaven (Philippians 3:20-21). In doing so they echoed the heart-cry of all the saints down through the ages from patriarchs to prophets who longed for the 'eternal city' (Hebrews 11:8-10, 16,

25-26, 39-40).

A healthy appreciation of our new and eternal ι.ο. not only helps us view the world better but it allows to even rise above it and ultimately embrace it all. For New Testament believers their new identity was rooted in the person of Jesus Christ through whom they had died and were now living as a new creation. Because of their union with Christ they had become largely disenfranchised on earth and were now free to love all humanity irrespective of social and economic distinctions. It was this same freedom in Christ and a proper understanding of things future that motivated them to reach everyone with the redeeming gospel of Christ (2 Corinthians 5:9-21).

Conclusion

The fact that eschatology plays a critical role in the Christian faith is indisputable. The sheer number of prophetic passages aside, the central role that prophecy plays in affirming God's Word and character is of utmost importance. Along with the death and resurrection of Christ his second coming and the ultimate consummation of all things under the headship of Christ are an essential part of the gospel message. The 'blessed hope' promised throughout Scriptures gives our faith a clear and specific goal.

Although discussions and debates on eschatological minutia will certainly continue up until the Lord's return, this should not discourage us from delving into the details and trying by God's grace to see the picture more fully. We should do this not merely out of theological curiosity but rather out of obedience and even more so out of a genuine desire to 'hasten' the day of the Lord. God's Word is emphatic that we need to be in the know regarding God's plan for the ages.

Two thousand years ago Jesus Christ entered Jerusalem on the foal of a donkey. In doing so he was fulfilling a number of prophecies regarding the long-awaited Messiah (Zechariah 9:9). Although the common folk were delighted to welcome him, the religious leaders made their repudiation of Jesus abundantly clear. In the face of such stubborn refusal, Christ was driven to tears. He wept because he knew of God's impending judgment on Israel on account of their rejection. He also wept because the prophecies of his coming had been so clear and yet they refused to recognize 'the time of his visitation' (Luke 19:28-44). Earlier Jesus had asked a question to the Jews that is just as pertinent to us today: *'When the Son of Man comes, will he find faith on the earth?'* (Luke 18:8).

A healthy understanding of Biblical eschatology is essential not just to prepare us for Christ's return but it also serves to motivate us in holy living, sacrificial service and vibrant disciple-making. A proper appreciation of the last days should transform our perspective on life and the world we live in. Moreover it should help us embrace our identity in Christ as exiles and sojourners on this earth. However, in order to succeed in this great marathon of faith it is imperative that we have a clear picture of the goal. Thus, we now turn our attention to the great Biblical theme of the kingdom.

2. THE KINGDOM

Have you ever attempted to put together a 10,000-piece puzzle? Just the sight of thousands of little odd shaped pieces strewn out before you is enough to make you want to walk away. In a similar way a glance at the myriads of verses relating to the last days can leave us feeling overwhelmed. However, when working on a puzzle it is useful to frequently refer back to the picture on the box to know what the puzzle is suppose to look like in the end. Secondly, it is important to start by putting the edge and corner pieces together in order to establish the general outline of the puzzle and then work yourself towards the middle. In a similar way before delving into all the details of Biblical eschatology we do well to keep the final picture in view and start by establishing the general framework of the perimeter.

When it comes to the end times, the promised kingdom constitutes the 'big picture.' Tracing God's plans with regard to this kingdom from creation down to its restoration at the end of human history, provides us the general outline needed to begin to make sense of the rest of our eschatology. Understanding the Scripture's teaching on the kingdom is essential if we hope to make any sense of the end times' puzzle.

As straightforward as this may seem, there are many different schools of interpretation regarding this foundational subject. Some like myself may have grown up in the 'dispensational' side of the aisle where all of redemption history is divided up into clear cut time periods in which God deals with mankind distinctly. 'Covenant' theologians on the other hand, largely reject such divisions and instead like to stress the overall thrust and unity in God's purposes down through history. Typical of such theological debates opposing groups tend to mischaracterize each other and present their own interpretation in contrast to the other one. This is unfortunate because in doing so we are no longer seeking a balanced Scriptural position but merely championing our own biased interpretation. Sadly such 'reactionary' theology leads to 'knee-jerk' interpretations put forth simply to counter the opposing side. But who said we need to take sides?

As usual, the truth is often somewhere in the middle. My experience is that both sides of the aisle have important contributions to make to the discussion but these are usually ignored when coming from the 'wrong' side. We do well to listen attentively to all parties while being careful to keep ourselves well grounded in the Biblical text. Ultimately God's truth should be our exegetical compass not the school of interpretation we represent. Otherwise we will find ourselves inadvertently trying to force verses to fit our particular eschatological framework instead of allowing God's Word to light our path.

Although we might still be unclear on the details, from the outset getting the general outline of our eschatology in place is essential. This will allow us to fill in the gaps with greater ease. Also, the end times' picture we are looking to as a guide will ultimately determine not just our eschatology but it will greatly influence the rest of our Christian theology and practice. As noted earlier, our understanding of the end times is not just a tag along optional theology, rather it leads the way for the other doctrines.

For example if we believe, like post-millennialists taught before WWII and many Christians under other names still espouse today, that with the right social and political reforms the world can be transformed so that we usher in the kingdom of God, then that will undoubtedly influence and shape our Christian ministry. If like others, we believe that no amount of praying and ministering will affect any real change in our doomed world, that we need to just sit tight waiting for Jesus to return and 'fix' everything, then we will succumb to spiritual laziness and ultimately fatalism. Again, the truth is usually somewhere in the middle. For this we need to remain teachable and stay Biblically balanced letting the Holy Spirit lead the way forward.

The Gospel Of The Kingdom

God's plans for the ages put forward by the Scriptures is best encapsulated in its teaching on the kingdom. The kingdom theme runs like a golden thread through the Bible from Genesis to Revelation. The preeminence of this theme is highlighted best by the Lord Jesus himself. And yet, though it constitutes the heart of Christ's message in the gospels, most modern believers hardly appreciate its significance and often fail to understand its grand scheme.

A cursory glance through the book of Matthew alone will reveal more than 50 references to the kingdom. Both John the Baptist and Jesus Christ make the subject of the kingdom central to their teaching. Here are a few familiar instances:

- Mat 3:2 - *"Repent, for the kingdom of heaven is at hand."*
- Mat 4:23 - *And he went throughout all Galilee, teaching in their synagogues and proclaiming the gospel of the kingdom*
- Mat 5:3 - *"Blessed are the poor in spirit, for theirs is the kingdom of heaven."*
- Mat 6:33 - *"But seek first the kingdom of God and his righteousness, and all these things will be added to you."*
- Mat 8:11 - *"I tell you, many will come from east and west and recline at table with Abraham, Isaac, and Jacob in the kingdom of heaven."*
- Mat 10:7 - *"And proclaim as you go, saying, 'The kingdom of heaven is at hand.'"*

- Mat 13:11 - *And he answered them, "To you it has been given to know the secrets of the kingdom of heaven, but to them it has not been given."*
- Mat 13:43 - *"Then the righteous will shine like the sun in the kingdom of their Father. He who has ears, let him hear."*
- Mat 18:4 - *"Whoever humbles himself like this child is the greatest in the kingdom of heaven."*
- Mat 24:14 - *"And this gospel of the kingdom will be proclaimed throughout the whole world as a testimony to all nations, and then the end will come."*

For Jesus the kingdom of God was not just some spiritual state or hyperbolic expression. He clearly taught that the kingdom was at hand, present and real. However it is also evident that the fuller elements of the kingdom he spoke of awaited a yet future fulfillment. Scholars have dubbed this the 'here but not yet' teaching. Ironically, although many modern believers are clueless of the kingdom, Christ's repeated allusions to the kingdom as he preached to the Jewish people of his day makes it clear that he were speaking of something innately familiar to them. Thus, in order to get the fuller picture of the kingdom we must go back to the beginning of Scriptures.

The Old Testament is replete with verses that emphasize God's ultimate sovereignty over the affairs of the earth (Psalms 9:7, 103:19). We see this worked out in the trial of Job, where the tempter is allowed to assail God's servant only to the extent that God permits it. This is because dominion ultimately belongs to God (Job 25:2). Later the pagan king of Babylon reluctantly came to the same conclusion after being humbled by the Most High.

At the end of the days I, Nebuchadnezzar, lifted my eyes to heaven, and my reason returned to me, and I blessed the Most High, and praised and honored him who lives forever, for his dominion is an everlasting dominion, and his kingdom endures from generation to generation (Daniel 4:34).

And yet, one glance down through the corridors of time and

across the planet today make it abundantly clear that while God may be the ultimate Lord of all, humankind is in open rebellion to him and his good earth in utter chaos. How is it that God's beautiful kingdom has fallen to its current condition? To see the fuller picture we need to start at the beginning.

The Original Kingdom

The kingdom theme is as old as the universe itself; it starts in the first chapter of the Bible. After creating the cosmos, God focused all his creative energy on our planet. Like a mother readying a room for her yet unborn child, God was in fact uniquely equipping planet earth so that his children, who will bear his image, can thrive therein. In short the whole of creation was uniquely designed for humans.[3]

As soon as he created mankind in the final day of creation, he tasked them with having dominion over every living creature. A couple of verses later he repeats this with a command: *"Be fruitful and multiply and fill the earth and subdue it, and have dominion..."* Clearly human beings are not just another species of animals, rather they were established as God's vice-regents on the kingdom of earth, uniquely equipped to rule and reign in his stead.

Chapter 2 of Genesis further stresses man's role as ruler of the planet when he is tasked with caring for the Garden of Eden. God took it even a step further by parading all the animals before man and granting him the privilege of naming them all. The unique authority of mankind over all creation could not be made any clearer. This message is not lost on the psalmist King David who writes the following with a profound sense of wonder:

When I look at your heavens, the work of your fingers, the moon and the stars, which you have set in place, what is man that you are mindful of him, and the son of man that you care for him?

Yet you have made him a little lower than the heavenly beings and crowned him with glory and honor. You have given him dominion over the works of your hands; you have put all things under his feet, all sheep and oxen, and also the beasts of the field, the birds of the heavens, and the fish of the sea, whatever passes along the paths of the seas (Psalm 8:3-8).

David clearly sees man as supreme commander and chief of the earth. According to the most ancient Masoretic texts, he actually describes man as *"a little lower than God."* That is a startling statement! In other words man was created second only to God himself in authority and dignity.

Centuries later the author of the letter to the Hebrews quotes this very same psalm. However he follows it up with some illuminating comments: *"Now in putting everything in subjection to him, he left nothing outside his control. At present, we do not yet see everything in subjection to him"* (Hebrews 2:8). First he reiterates that mankind was originally put in supreme control of the earth. However he then points out the obvious fact that mankind no longer seem to be in control of his environment, in fact, everything seems to have spiraled out of control. How and when did that happen?

The Kingdom Falls

Genesis chapter 3 introduces us to a strange creature, a talking serpent. Scriptures subsequently reveal its identity as none other than Satan, the devil himself (Revelation 12). The archenemy of God approaches the woman in the Garden of Eden enticing her to eat of the forbidden fruit. He is intent on casting a shadow on God's character and urging our ancestors to join him in rebellion against God. He is ultimately seeking to usurp their right to rule in God's earthly kingdom.

We learn from other passages that Satan was originally created as a high-ranking angel, an 'anointed cherub'. Yet at some point 'unrighteousness was found in him' and he became corrupted (Ezekiel 28:13-19). In the same passage we also read that he was in Eden, in his uncorrupted form. What happened there that caused him to fall? Interestingly the Islamic version of this same event draws on earlier Rabbinic oral traditions claiming that upon creating man, God commanded the angelic hosts to bow before him. Lucifer upon refusing to do so was thrown out of God's presence.[4]

The veracity of these stories surrounding the fall of Satan is highly questionable, if anything because it makes the devil out to be the victim. However, it does force us to reckon with the question of how the great anointed cherub fell. The fact that Lucifer was in the Garden of Eden before he fell into sin does make us wonder if the unique privilege given to man had a role in making him envious. Ezekiel 28:12 calls Lucifer the 'signet of perfection, full of wisdom and perfect in beauty.' Then the passage goes on to describe him as being covered with all manner of luxurious gems, almost reminiscent of the High Priest. Eden is further described as the 'holy mountain of God' which again foreshadows the New Jerusalem and the temple in Zion. In a very real sense heaven and earth were in perfect harmony in the original creation.

From the few details afforded us by Ezekiel we can surmise that Lucifer held a very prominent position in the Garden of Eden. Usually cherubs are assigned to God's throne but he was uniquely tasked with 'covering' or 'guarding' God's children in the new earthly kingdom. This new world was one of remarkable beauty and complete harmony. Genesis hints at the fact that God regularly visited and communed with Adam and Eve in the garden. One day however, this glorious chorus of joy and peace came to an abrupt halt.

What exactly triggered Lucifer's downfall remains for the time a mystery, however the fact that he immediately sought to bring humanity down with him seems to indicate some measure of envy. Also the fact that he comes in the form of a serpent is likely because he has been dispossessed of his angelic vestments and authority. Thus, he seems to be coveting the dominion that has been entrusted to mankind. Tragically, he succeeds in convincing the humans to abandon their child-like trust in God and rise up in rebellion. Thus, rather than guarding God's children he corrupted their innocence and stole their inheritance.

In the immediate fallout of human sin, man and woman felt deep shame and fear for the first time. When God confronted them, instead of repenting, they resorted to the blame-game. Ultimately Satan is found to be the culprit but humans are not absolved. In dolling out their punishments, God makes a point of establishing a distinction between mankind and the devil. Although Satan may have hoped to have humans as his allies against God, the Lord stresses that there will be enmity between them until the day that the promised 'Seed' comes to crush the head of the serpent (Genesis 3:15). This enigmatic promise sets the stage for the great struggle between humankind and satanic forces that would ultimately come to a head in the incarnation.

The following verses highlight the chaos brought on by sin and rebellion. The original human institution, marriage, is corrupted so that enmity between husband and wife ensue. Moreover, the relationship between man and the earthly kingdom with which he was entrusted, is now cursed by sin resulting in death (Romans 5;12-14). Worse, the effects of their revolt will ultimately infect the whole realm of creation (Romans 8:19-22). Most importantly mankind's relationship with God is ruptured as they are expelled from the lush gardens of Eden.

The Kingdom Of Babylon

With the fall of mankind, the God-appointed ruler is no longer at the helm, rather he has become a subject of Satan. In obeying the devil he has forfeited his right to rule, even worse, he has turned the reins over to Satan. This is why the Scriptures often speak of Satan as the ruler of this present world:

- John 12:31 - *Now is the judgment of this world; now will the ruler of this world be cast out.*
- John 14:30 - *I will no longer talk much with you, for the ruler of this world is coming. He has no claim on me* (See also: John 16:11).
- 2 Corinthians 4:4 - *In their case the god of this world has blinded the minds of the unbelievers, to keep them from seeing the light of the gospel of the glory of Christ, who is the image of God.*
- Ephesians 2:1-2 - *And you were dead in the trespasses and sins in which you once walked, following the course of this world, following the prince of the power of the air, the spirit that is now at work in the sons of disobedience* (See also: Ephesians 6:12).
- 1 John 5:19 - *We know that we are from God, and the whole world lies in the power of the evil one.*

This is not to say that God is no longer sovereign over the affairs of man or that he has given up his rightful claim to the earth. However, man, who was entrusted with ruling the earth, by opening the door to Satan, ushered sin and death into the world. Thus, even though the cosmos remains within the ultimate boundaries of God's realm and authority, mankind's sin had paved the way for a dark insurrection that in a short time would engulf the globe.

The insidious effects of sin come to light in chapter 4 of Genesis when Cain, Adam's firstborn son, also falls prey to pride and envy going so far as to murder his own brother. He fails to master the evil one crouching at the door and is ultimately ruined by him. This leads to the eventual ruin of his descendants. This is best evidenced by the gross arrogance of Lamech, Cain's great grandson, who not only takes multiple wives but also boasts of killing a man wantonly, all the while flaunting God's judgment (Genesis 4:23-24).

Although not much is known of the generations from Adam to Noah, the few details available and the resulting judgment are enough to paint a harrowing backdrop. Firstly it is important to note that we are talking of roughly 1,500 years of human history. Secondly, humans are said to have lived an average of 900 years. Thirdly we are told that they had invented all types of musical instruments as well as learning to forge all manner of tools and weapons from bronze and iron (Genesis 4:21). These were no cave-men! There is no telling just how advanced the antediluvian civilization was, and yet, we are told that they became so corrupted that God was compelled to utterly wipe them from the planet with the flood (Genesis 6:5).

What happened that precipitated such a global calamity? Genesis chapter 6 gives us a short synopsis of the primary reason for the flood. Although few details are provided, it seems evident that some grotesque union between mankind and the demonic realm was ultimately responsible for the catastrophic deluge that ensued. Evil spirits somehow found a way of enticing and even impregnating women with the result that a type of half-breed race of giants (Nephilim) began to rule the earth. Consequently, because the race of man became irreparably corrupted God chose to destroy them all. Only Noah, who was pure and uncorrupted in his genealogy, was spared with his family.

On account of humankind subjugating themselves to Satan, the antediluvian world clearly came under demonic influence resulting in its complete destruction. After the flood, however, it did not take long for Satan to inspire a new generation of rulers to challenge God's authority again. This he did with Nimrod the 'Rebel' king of the Sumerian kingdom. The Bible describes him as a great hunter who set his face against God (Genesis 10:8-10). Many scholars believe that the legends of Gilgamesh can ultimately be traced back to Nimrod, the tyrannical king of Mesopotamia who claimed to be part god. The Jewish historian Josephus writes that Nimrod had a vendetta against God for destroying his forefathers in the flood. Thus he orchestrated the building of a great tower insulated with tar against a future deluge, rising up to heaven as a symbol of human defiance against the Almighty.[5]

The Biblical account of the tower of Babel is reminiscent of the first rebellion in the Garden of Eden. Mankind has been given a second chance to live in obedience to God and to subjugate the world, and yet instead they choose to rebel. *"Come, let us build ourselves a city and a tower with its top in the heavens, and let us make a name for ourselves, lest we be dispersed over the face of the whole earth"* (Genesis 11:4). Again it is human pride and a desire to be masters of their own fate and future that motivates their rebellion. Once again God is forced to intervene, partly in his grace, to disperse them rather than destroy them.

Although Satan is not directly mentioned in the account of Babel, he is clearly the driving force behind it. Thus it is not surprising that throughout Scriptures 'Babylon' is characterized as the epitome of Satan's kingdom, the great antitype of God's kingdom (Isaiah 14:3-13; Revelation 17-18). In Daniel's visions, Babylon heads up the litany of human empires in the Middle East that have stood against God's purposes; and yet they will all ultimately succumb to the eternal reign of the Son of Man (Daniel 2, 7).

In short, the Scriptures tell a tale of two kingdoms. The earthly branch of God's eternal kingdom is compromised by human rebellion and ultimately falls under the spell of Satan who uses it to establish his own kingdom. Thus various human attempts to rule the world down through history are seen as ultimately orchestrated by the devil and his dark forces who manipulate the powers that be to their own evil ends (Daniel 10:13, 20). But God will not surrender the kingdom of earth and mankind to Satan forever.

The Promised King

It is in light of the repeated and catastrophic failure of

mankind to live in obedience to God and the resulting Satanic deception rampant in the world, that we come upon the story of God's covenant with Abraham. God is seeking to establish a beach-head to begin his reconquest of the world. He calls Abram to leave behind the corrupted kingdom of Babylon and come to a new land where God will start laying again the foundation for his own kingdom. Even as he leaves behind his former country Abram was *'looking forward to the city that has foundations, whose designer and builder is God'* (Hebrews 11:10). Abram and his descendants were clearly eager to see God reestablish his heavenly kingdom on the earth once more.

Genesis 12 starts with God promising to make Abram into a great nation, a new kingdom. This new people of God are to counter the curse in the world by being a blessing to all nations, even as they are blessed in their relationship with God. Thus Abram's seed is featured as God's choice vessel of blessing and ultimate restoration. The 'seed' motif was not something new; it had been mentioned earlier to Adam and Eve when God promised that the 'seed of the woman' would crush the head of Satan.

From Abraham's seed or descendants, a new royal lineage begins to emerge (Genesis 17:6). God reveals himself and his purposes with more clarity to each successive generation even as he calls them to remain faithful to him and live in the promised land. On his deathbed as he blessed his sons, Jacob uttered another remarkable promise relevant to the promised kingdom: *"The scepter shall not depart from Judah, nor the ruler's staff from between his feet, until tribute (Shiloh) comes to him; and to him shall be the obedience of the peoples"* (Genesis 49:10). The word 'Shiloh' means 'the one to whom it is due' or 'the rightful owner.' From ancient times scholars have almost unanimously linked this term to the promised Messiah.[6] In this way the long-awaited king who will ultimately rule all nations is expected to come from the tribe of Judah (Revelation 5:5).

During the great famine in the time of Joseph the sons of Jacob migrated to Egypt where they ended up staying for over

400 years and becoming slaves of the Pharaoh. However God raised up his servant Moses to deliver them and usher them back to the land promised to Abraham. At Mount Sinai God met his chosen people with this important message:

> *You yourselves have seen what I did to the Egyptians, and how I bore you on eagles' wings and brought you to myself. Now therefore, if you will indeed obey my voice and keep my covenant, you shall be my treasured possession among all peoples, for all the earth is mine; and you shall be to me a kingdom of priests and a holy nation* (Exodus 19:4-6).

God's stated intent is to make Israel his chosen vessel of blessing for all the nations, a holy people, a kingdom of priests. As such he stresses that the whole of the earth ultimately belongs to him, but it is through his unique relationship with Israel that God plans to bring redemption to all mankind and win the earth back.

Now the nation of Israel was never wholly up to the task. Even after conquering the land of Canaan they repeatedly fell into idolatry. That until God raised up a righteous king for them, David, a man after God's own heart. It was with King David that God added another covenant in which he promised to preserve the Davidic dynasty and establish his kingdom forever. He further promised to raise up one of the kind's descendants to be the eternal king (2 Samuel 7:12-16). Numerous psalms echo this great kingdom theme (Psalm 2, 24, 45-48, 110). The prophets later picked up on this great promise of the coming king.

> *For to us a child is born, to us a son is given; and the government shall be upon his shoulder, and his name shall be called Wonderful Counselor, Mighty God, Everlasting. Of the increase of his government and of peace there will be no end, on the throne of David and over his kingdom, to establish it and to uphold it with justice and with righteousness from this time forth and forevermore. The zeal of the LORD of hosts will do this* (Isaiah 9:6-7).

Time and again God made it abundantly clear through the prophets that he would take back the kingdom of earth through his promised Messiah. Like the Garden of Eden, the kingdom once established will be a high mountain in the center of the earth to which all the nations will flock to pay homage to the Messiah (Micah 4:1-3). As in the original creation mankind and the animals will live in perfect peace and harmony in God's renewed earth (Isaiah 11:1-10). In the end, God promises to 'swallow up death' and finally and fully undo the effects of sin and corruption (Isaiah 25:8, 43:25).

This was the great and glorious expectation of the Jewish nation at the time of Jesus Christ. At that time they longed for the promised king to come and dismantle the Roman Empire and establish the nation of Israel at the head of all nations. It was into this highly politically charged environment that Jesus the Nazarene entered preaching the gospel of the kingdom. However the Jewish people were in for a surprise.

The Humble King

From the outset the life of Jesus was paradoxical. The Jews knew to expect the Messiah from the tribe of Judah, from the family of David, to be born in Bethlehem, however when the fullness of time came, they were completely caught off guard. Jesus, instead of being born to royalty, was born to a peasant family. The promised 'seed of the woman' came to fruition in the womb of a humble virgin, Mary. However Gabriel's pronouncement to her revealing the true identity of Jesus could not have been any clearer:

> *And behold, you will conceive in your womb and bear a son, and you shall call his name Jesus. He will be great and will be called the Son of the Most High. And the Lord God will give to him the throne of his father David, and he will reign over the house of Jacob forever, and of his kingdom there will be no end* (Luke

1:31-33).

The connection to the aforementioned kingdom promise made to David is unmistakable and yet here he was, the king of the world, lying in a manger. His first visitors were not the rulers or priests from nearby Jerusalem but rather common shepherds from the fields who came telling a wild tale of seeing an angel who claimed that the Messiah, the Lord himself, had been born in Bethlehem (Luke 2:1-20). Later when magi showed up from the east looking for the King, once again the elite in Jerusalem were totally caught off guard (Matthew 2:1-12).

The years passed by and the time finally came for Christ to begin his public ministry. This he did by being baptized by his relative John who had been proclaiming the Messiah's imminent arrival for some time. Then as Jesus was baptized the heavens opened and God's resounding voice proclaimed him to be the very Son of God even as the Holy Spirit descended upon him in the form of a dove. We often miss the fact that this was not just a baptism, rather it was a formal anointing ceremony.

The title 'Messiah' literally means 'the anointed one'. In the Old Testament priests, prophets and kings were anointed when they formally began their public ministry. Christ, who was to combine all the chief offices in himself, is here anointed under the auspices of John the greatest prophet, with both the confirming presence of the Holy Spirit and the affirming voice of God the Father. Furthermore the designation he received, 'Son of God,' clearly harks back to the Messianic title endowed on the promised King (Psalm 2).

As the newly anointed King, what would we expect Jesus to do? Interestingly instead of fomenting a rebellion against Rome he starts by going to the wilderness where he takes on the real seat of power, the devil himself. Unlike the first Adam who quickly fell for Satan's schemes, Jesus proves to be more than up to the task. From his interchange with the enemy it is clear Satan knows why Jesus has shown up. The devil knows Jesus has come for the kingdom, so he offers him a short-cut: 'Just bow to me and the kingdom is yours!' Jesus however does not take the bait.

In his subsequent three years of ministry the cosmic battle between Jesus and the devil intensifies. Christ begins to dismantle Satan's reign of terror by casting out demons, healing the sick and raising the dead. The devil for his part begins to mobilize the religious elite against Jesus to try to discredit his ministry and ultimately destroy his efforts to deliver the people from the kingdom of darkness. All the while Jesus continues to proclaim the good news of the kingdom. Some of the people hope this means the end to Roman oppression but Jesus refuses to be drawn into a political firestorm and instead continues to call people to repentance and spiritual transformation.

This epic struggle comes to a head when Jesus comes to Jerusalem for the Passover festival. Although he had repeatedly refused to come out publicly as the Messiah, on this occasion he personally orchestrates the fulfillment of Zechariah's prophecy regarding the promised King. *"Rejoice greatly, O daughter of Zion! Shout aloud, O daughter of Jerusalem! Behold, your king is coming to you; righteous and having salvation is he, humble and mounted on a donkey, on a colt, the foal of a donkey"* (Zechariah 9:9).

Even though the common people gladly welcomed Jesus as their promised King, the Jewish leadership made it abundantly clear that they refused to acknowledge him as their Messiah. In light of their overt rejection Jesus told the parable of the landowner in which the tenants, who represent the Jews, kill the heir of the kingdom in an attempt to keep the vineyard for themselves. The Lord ends with this severe indictment of Israel: *"Therefore I tell you, the kingdom of God will be taken away from you and given to a people producing its fruits"* (Matthew 21:43). Not only does Jesus predict his death in advance but he also speaks to the next phase of the kingdom.

In the ensuing chapters it becomes evident that the literal kingdom promised to Israel is off the table, at least for the time being. In fact, Jesus, after listing the hypocrisies of the Jewish ruling establishment, speaks to the imminent destruction of the temple and the yet future tribulation. Only when his people acknowledge their sin and welcome him back does Jesus promise to return in glory to establish his kingdom.

Soon afterwards Jesus is betrayed by one of his own, then he is arrested and brought before the high priest. Despite many desperate attempts to frame him they are ultimately forced to address the heart of the issue. Thus the high priest puts Jesus under oath and asks if he is indeed the promised Messiah, the Son of God. Jesus, not only respond affirmatively, he goes further by directly linking himself to the 'Son of Man' prophesied in Daniel 7 who is to receive the promised kingdom from God. The scandalized Jewish leaders reject his claim out of hand and take him to the Roman authorities to be crucified.

When questioned by Pilate again the subject of the kingdom arises and Jesus does not deny that he is a king. However he makes it clear that his kingdom is not an imminent threat to the political power of Rome at that time. Thus it is with sarcastic irony that Pilate has the indictment, *"Jesus King of the Jews"* written above his cross.

The Kingdom Is At Hand

From beginning to end the life and ministry of Jesus Christ is framed in the context of the long-awaited kingdom. And although Satan seemed to defeat him at the cross, Jesus had the final word when he rose victoriously, defeating death and crushing the head of the serpent. Soon afterwards once he had regathered his disciples he announced that *'all authority in heaven and on earth has been given to me.'* (Matthew 28:18). With this statement he is emphatically proclaiming that he has won back the right to rule the earth again. Having vanquished the devil the next step is to reunite heaven and earth under the kingdom of God.

Later as he prepares to ascend to the right hand of the Father's throne, his disciples inquire further about the imminent establishment of the kingdom: *"Lord, will you at this time restore the kingdom to Israel?"* In his response Jesus reiterates that the actual timing of the fulfillment of that promise rests with the Father alone. In the meantime he urges his disciples to prepare for the task at hand, namely, witnessing of the gospel to all the nations. Soon afterwards Jesus is taken up in the clouds. As the disciples stand awestruck a pair of angels appears reminding them that Christ will return to finish what he had started (Acts 1:8-11).

At this point many erroneously assume that the promise of the kingdom has been completely removed from the cards. However a quick survey of the book of Acts makes it abundantly clear that the apostles still very much believed in the historical fulfillment of the kingdom (Acts 8:12, 14:22, 19:8, 20:25, 28:23, 31). They regularly connect Jesus to the Davidic covenant and the promised earthly reign (Acts 2:30). They further view his ascension and enthronement in heaven as a temporary dispensation awaiting his future return and kingdom (Acts 2:33-36). Peter's second sermon best summarizes their expectation:

> *Repent therefore, and turn back, that your sins may be blotted out, that times of refreshing may come from the presence of the Lord, and that he may send the Christ appointed for you, Jesus, whom heaven must receive until the time for restoring all the things about which God spoke by the mouth of his holy prophets long ago* (Acts 3:19-21).

In speaking to his own people Peter clearly believes that their national repentance would trigger the return of the Messiah and the awaited restoration of the kingdom. A brief tour of the apostolic letters highlights their continued allegiance to the gospel of the kingdom proclaimed by Jesus and the prophets before him.

- Romans 14:17 - *For the kingdom of God is not a matter of eating and drinking but of righteousness and peace and joy in the Holy Spirit.*

- 1 Corinthians 4:20 - *For the kingdom of God does not consist in talk but in power.*
- 1 Corinthians 6:9-10 - *Or do you not know that the unrighteous will not inherit the kingdom of God? Do not be deceived: neither the sexually immoral, nor idolaters, nor adulterers, nor men who practice homosexuality, nor thieves, nor the greedy, nor drunkards, nor revilers, nor swindlers will inherit the kingdom of God* (See also: Galatians 5:21, Ephesians 5:5).
- 1 Thessalonians 2:12 - *We exhorted each one of you and encouraged you and charged you to walk in a manner worthy of God, who calls you into his own kingdom and glory.*
- 2 Thessalonians 1:5 - *This is evidence of the righteous judgment of God, that you may be considered worthy of the kingdom of God, for which you are also suffering.*
- 2 Timothy 4:1 - *I charge you in the presence of God and of Christ Jesus, who is to judge the living and the dead, and by his appearing and his kingdom...*
- 2 Timothy 4:18 - *The Lord will rescue me from every evil deed and bring me safely into his heavenly kingdom. To him be the glory forever and ever. Amen.*
- Hebrews 12:28 - *Therefore let us be grateful for receiving a kingdom that cannot be shaken, and thus let us offer to God acceptable worship, with reverence and awe.*
- James 2:5 - *Listen, my beloved brothers, has not God chosen those who are poor in the world to be rich in faith and heirs of the kingdom, which he has promised to those who love him?*
- 2 Peter 1:11 - *For in this way there will be richly provided for you an entrance into the eternal kingdom of our Lord and Savior Jesus Christ.*

From the above passages it is clear that the apostles see both a present and yet future fulfillment to the promised kingdom. Paul expresses the present nature of the kingdom quite forcefully in Colossians 1:13 - '*He has delivered us from the domain of darkness and transferred us to the kingdom of his beloved*

Son.' There is no denying that the kingdom promises have in some form begun to be fulfilled in the church age because Christ has already received all authority in heaven and earth. Even now the blessings of the gospel are reaching all nations. However it would be a grave mistake to simply spiritualize the remaining literal promises connected to the kingdom and assume that the church has it covered. Quite to the contrary, Jesus himself taught his disciples to pray, *"Your kingdom come, your will be done on earth as it is in heaven."* Thus we await the fullness of the kingdom to be realized when Christ returns and reigns over all the earth from the throne of David.

Finally the book of Revelation further highlights this 'here but not yet' nature of the kingdom. Some passages speak of God having 'made us a kingdom' and of 'the suffering in tribulation for the sake of the kingdom' (Revelation 1:6, 9, 5:10). However as the Revelation progresses towards the conclusion, namely the glorious return of Christ, it stresses the yet future restoration of the earthly kingdom to God's kingdom, *"The kingdom of the world has become the kingdom of our Lord and of his Christ, and he shall reign forever and ever"* (Revelation 11:15). This is finally realized when Satan, the great deceiver, loses control of the heavenlies and is sent down to earth to await his final demise at the hand of Christ (Revelation 12:10). At that time the Lord Jesus will descend and take his seat on the throne of David and rule over the whole earth for 1,000 years along with all the resurrected believers who will reign with him (Revelation 20:1-6).

Conclusion

The theme of the kingdom best encapsulates the overall message of the Scriptures. It is the Biblical metanarrative; the skeleton on which all the covenants and promises are wonderfully woven together. Keeping our eyes on the panoramic picture of the kingdom is essential to a well-rounded eschatology, because it focuses our attention on the consummation of redemption history, namely the vindication of God's eternal purposes.

The original world that God created was entrusted to the care of mankind. Adam and Eve were the rulers of the glorious kingdom of earth. Satan, however, succeeded in luring them into joining his rebellion, so that with the fall of man their kingdom also fell into his hands. Thus the current state of affairs is one in which God's glorious creation has been highjacked by the devil.

But paradise is not lost forever, rather its restoration is predicted from the outset and throughout the Old Testament the way is paved for the rightful ruler to return. Patriarchs and prophets all look forward to the time when the Lord would once again reign supreme on the earth. The nation of Israel is uniquely chosen as a catalyst for the restoration of the kingdom. The promised king is expected to bring an end to all futile efforts of human governance inspired as they are by Satan and restore humanity to their position of preeminence.

At the fullness of time, when the king finally arrives on the stage of human history he takes the fight straight to Satan. In the subsequent battle of wills the Lord Jesus begins to dismantle the devil's reign of terror. However the enemy succeeds in arousing the envy of the Jewish leaders so that they kill their own Messiah. And yet, even as he deals a lethal blow to the king, he receives a crushing blow to the head when Christ rises from the dead.

The Kingdom of God

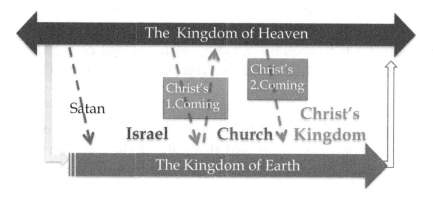

The battle is won and the right to reign belongs to the God-man Christ Jesus but the ramifications of his victory will take time to materialize. The king is first taken up to heaven to begin his heavenly reign pending the fulfillment of his earthly kingdom. At this time the gospel of the kingdom is preached to all the nations, calling all to repentance and faith in the Savior. The nation of Israel is also called to national repentance in order to finally usher in the return of the Messiah. In the end the enemies of God will be utterly defeated and the Lord Jesus will return to earth to claim the Davidic throne (Hosea 3:4-5). Then Christ will reign on earth for 1,000 years at the end of which the kingdom of earth will finally be returned to the kingdom of His Father (1 Corinthians 15:23-28).

While most Christians recognize the essential nature of the kingdom theme in Scriptures, there are still markedly different interpretations of this crucial subject that lead to very different outcomes. Some focus on the literal promises made to Israel and insist on their literal fulfillment after the return of Christ. Thus when speaking of the kingdom they tend to focus solely on the ultimate 1,000 year reign of Christ on earth as predicted by the prophets. Others focus on the spiritual dimension of the kingdom theme stressing the current heavenly reign of Christ exercised through his people on earth. Because of this their tendency is to allegorize any specific references to a yet future reign of Christ on earth.

Before taking sides it is important to ask if these two approaches are really mutually exclusive. Taken in their extreme forms they do seem incompatible, but if we seek a more Biblically balanced middle-ground I believe we can hold them in proper tension. Firstly it is vital to stress the importance of approaching the Biblical text with complete trust and respect. Where it gives us detailed information about things yet future I believe we need to honor God's revelation and refrain from over-spiritualizing them. At the same time those of us who tend to gravitate to a more straight-forward or literal interpretation of the text do well to also appreciate the overarching kingdom paradigm and its present spiritual dimension.

When it comes to the kingdom instead of taking an "*either/or*" approach, namely either present/spiritual or future/literal, we can see a "*both/and*" fulfillment. In other words, we need to stress both Christ's current reign from heaven and the culmination of his kingdom when he returns to reign on earth. From a Biblical standpoint we can see that his kingdom was indeed inaugurated in his first coming and he is now reigning over his people from heaven, yet we must also recognize that the yet unfulfilled promises related to his earthly kingdom will indeed become a reality in his second coming.

3. THE REMNANT

For the past couple of decades I've lived in the land of conspiracies. In the Middle East whenever there is any great catastrophe, whether financial or political, it won't take long for people to start pointing the finger at Israel. Even natural disasters are regularly blamed on the seemingly omnipotent and omniscient influence of the Jews. Indeed, no nation on earth has played a more polarizing role in human history than Israel. This is particularly and often painfully evident in the Middle East.

Anti-semitism is an integral part of the Islamic world-view because the Jews are portrayed as the arch rivals of Muslims. Their prophet initially curried the favor of the Jewish community in Mecca trying to prove to them that he was a messenger of God akin to other Biblical prophets. The first Muslim community adopted many Jewish rituals including ceremonial washings, fasts and daily prayers. In fact in the earliest period of their history, Muslims did their prayers facing Jerusalem. However, upon being rejected and denounced as a false prophet by the Jews, Mohammed took his movement to Medina where he changed tactic and soon began persecuting Jews in the vicinity. So it was that Jewry gained the unmitigated enmity of Islam.

However, it must also be noted that the anti-semitism phenomena is not limited to Muslim nations, in fact, it has an even longer and equally tragic history in the context of Christendom. It is important to recognize that anti-semitism's most notorious example, the Holocaust, has its roots in flawed Christian theology so that to this day Jews blame the followers of Yeshua for their near-annihilation at the hands of the Nazis. Sadly, the underpinnings of this errant theological framework are still latent and even resurgent under the name 'replacement theology.' Proponents of this notion essentially believe that the church has supplanted Israel in God's plan of redemption.

This theological view has been known historically as 'supersessionism' and has been rebranded more recently as 'fulfillment theology.' It is thought that because the Jewish nation rejected Jesus as their Messiah they were cursed and permanently removed from God's redemptive plan being replaced ultimately by the universal church. Adherents of this view largely base this on the notion that the New Covenant has unequivocally superseded the Old Covenant. Understanding the correlation between the Old and New Testaments is not an easy matter, however, concluding that Israel no longer has any role to play in the eternal purposes of God clearly contradicts many New Testament passages. More importantly taking such 'replacement' notions to their logical conclusions has opened the door to many abuses against Jewry down through history.

The first signs of 'supersessionism' began to appear in the writings of the church fathers in the second and third century. At that time, because Christianity was still largely a minority group and often maligned by its Jewish counterparts, early church leaders often saw Jews as rivals if not as enemies. Also, the fact that the nation of Israel had rejected Jesus as their Messiah and had suffered the judgments predicted by Jesus, led many Christians to view them as cursed. Thus by the time of the Council of Nicea, when Christianity was gaining prominence across the empire, the Jews were increasingly viewed unfavorably.

Just prior to this time the allegorical interpretations of respected teacher and prolific author Origen of Alexandria began to pave the way for a spiritualized reinterpretation of the Old Testament. His hermeneutical methods, influenced greatly by the Greek philosophy of his day, as well as the latent contempt towards Jews, led him to effectively disinherit the nation of Israel. In the ensuing centuries, as Christianity became wedded with the Roman Empire, the characterization of the church as the new and improved Israel became more popular. This anti-semitic sentiment was further promulgated by prominent church spokesmen like Ambrose and ultimately popularized by the great Augustine of Hippo.

> "It is a fact of history that the Augustinian concept of a Christian theocracy is closely linked with the anti-Semitic attitudes of the medieval church and unbelievably harsh treatment of the Jewish people."[7]

The litany of abuses directed towards the Jewish people by none other than the church of Christ, has left an abominable stain on our history. As easy as it might be to point the finger at the Catholic Church of the Middle Ages, we should note that even the great Martin Luther at times echoed the anti-semitic sentiments of his day.

Thus we are brought back to the pressing question: What should we believe with regards to Israel in light of the New Covenant? Since the establishment of the modern nation of Israel in 1948 many evangelicals have flocked to the support of Jews, some to the extent of behaving as if the state of Israel can do no wrong. Now, as exciting as the restoration of Jewish people to their historical homeland may be, we clearly need to find our Biblical balance in this matter as well.

Jesus And The Jews

For those of us who believe in the Scriptures, God's choice of Abraham and his seed, the nation of Israel, as his chosen people is beyond dispute. However, we understand that he did this not for their own sake, but that they might be a blessing and a light to all the nations of the earth. This promise found its fulfillment in the ultimate 'Seed' of Abraham, the Lord Jesus Christ (Galatians 3:16). In order to fulfill these predictions it was essential for Jesus to be born a Jew. In fact, the first verses of the New Testament, take great pains to establish the Jewish lineage of Jesus Christ (Matthew 1).

Jesus clearly loved his nation and went to great lengths to reach them with the gospel of the kingdom. In fact, by refusing to serve those outside of Israel, he made his commitment to his people's redemption abundantly clear. However, even as the common people flocked to him and hung on his every word, it did not take long for the religious establishment to become envious of his success. This led to some heated interchanges between Jesus and the leaders in which he noted that they were behaving more like the children of the devil than as the children of their father Abraham (John 8:44).

On rare occasions Jesus did take his gospel to the neighbors of Israel, most notably the Samaritans. In one such instance his exchange with the woman at the well is particularly instructive. After pointing out her moral deficiency she reacts by stoking the flames of ethnic rivalry between Jews and Samaritans. Jesus responds as follows:

> *Woman, believe me, the hour is coming when neither on this mountain nor in Jerusalem will you worship the Father. You worship what you do not know; we worship what we know, **for salvation is from the Jews**. But the hour is coming, and is now here, when the true worshipers will worship the Father in spirit and truth, for the Father is seeking such people to worship him* (John 4:21-23).

He first points out that our place of birth and religious heritage should not dictate our faith because ultimately all nations are welcome to worship God in spirit. However he tempers this by also stressing that our worship must be rooted in truth. In other words, we must come to an accurate understanding of who God is in order to truly worship him. But where is this knowledge to be found? Jesus' forthright answer is, 'salvation is from the Jews.' In short, the only way to true knowledge of God is by appreciating his historic revelation to Israel in the Old Testament.

Christ's statement is a far cry from the postmodern relativistic gibberish of our day in which everyone is urged to approach God on his/her own terms. Jesus insists that faith must be rooted in fact, and the fact is that our knowledge of the one true God is contingent on accepting his revelation to the Jews. Outside of the Bible, any comprehensive understanding of God and his purposes is impossible. Likewise open contempt for Israel is incompatible with genuine faith in Christ.

In the subsequent months, despite providing abundant evidence to back up his Messianic claims, the Jewish leadership categorically deny the Lord Jesus and he begins the long journey to the cross. In his last days he tells a number of parables that stress the temporary postponement of his kingdom agenda pending his glorious return (Luke 19:11-27). He also notes that in the meantime, the kingdom of God will be taken from Israel and entrusted to another who will bring it to fruition (Matthew 21:33-46). This clear reference to the church should not be misunderstood to mean the eventual replacement of Israel because in the subsequent chapters Jesus speaks to the ultimate restoration of Israel to God's purposes.

In chapter 24 of Matthew Jesus mentions the impending destruction of Jerusalem and the temple because of their rejection of the Messiah. Upon further inquiry by the disciples about this prophecy and his second coming Jesus responds with a detailed description of two interrelated events. The first is the imminent destruction of the temple fulfilled in 70 A.D. The second relates to a yet future desecration of the temple leading up to the glorious return of the Messiah. Both of these events are preceded by periods of great distress and persecution. However the fact that Christ did not return after the first destruction of the temple makes it clear that a second destruction is to be expected. For this the temple needs to be built again, which necessitates the restoration of the scattered people of Israel to their historic land.

Right in the middle of this discourse Jesus interestingly urges them to remember the parable of the fig tree.

> *From the fig tree learn its lesson: as soon as its branch becomes tender and puts out its leaves, you know that summer is near. So also, when you see all these things, you know that he is near, at the very gates. Truly, I say to you, this generation will not pass away until all these things take place. Heaven and earth will pass away, but my words will not pass away* (Matthew 24:32-35).

It is important to note that the word translated 'generation' here (Gr: genea), can refer not just to a people from a particular period of time but also to people from a particular ethnic group, namely a specific clan or nation.[8] This is likely a double entendre meant to emphasize that the events in question would take place in the life-span of those hearing Jesus but also that the nation of Israel would survive such tribulations to see its ultimate fulfillment. This hints at the apparent 'indestructibility' of the Jewish nation, because God is not finished with them yet.

Going back to the parable of the fig tree, we might recall that Jesus had previously had a peculiar experience with a barren fig tree. At that time his disciples had been mystified by his rebuke and subsequent curse of the fruitless tree. Most interpreters note that this is likely a pictorial reference to Israel's lack of fruit and resulting curse. However, there is likely more to this parable, namely, that when Jesus tells his disciples to keep their eyes on the fig tree, he is in fact telling us to look for the fruit of repentance in the nation of Israel as a key sign of his return. When Israel shows signs of repentance we can be sure that the Lord's appearing is near.

The Jewish Church

After Christ's glorious resurrection Jesus evidently had several discussions with his disciples regarding the kingdom of God. In this context when his disciples asked him, 'is it at this time that you will restore the kingdom to Israel', we get a clear picture of their expectation with regard to the future of the promised kingdom. The disciples cannot envisage a kingdom that does not involve the nation of Israel to whom the promises were originally given. Likewise Jesus in his response does not in any way lead them to expect anything different. However he does imply that in the interim they are tasked with a global mission (Acts 1:3-8).

Soon afterwards on the day of Pentecost the Holy Spirit is poured out on the disciples and the age of the church is launched. The parallels of this momentous event with the covenant made with Israel at Sinai are striking. There is a violent rushing wind and earthquake as fire from heaven descends upon them. This is the commencement of the New Covenant, but unlike the covenant at Sinai where only Moses was deemed worthy of entering God's presence, after Pentecost every believer is filled with God's Spirit and experiences God's miraculous power at work in them.[9]

God was in a way reformatting his people Israel, this time around 12 apostles instead of 12 tribes. But notice that this was still very much a Jewish enterprise as the church was entirely made up of Jews. This should not surprise us as the New Covenant was likewise made to the nation of Israel (Jeremiah 31:31-34). The difference though was that now all the nations would come to know God through them because God had provided a means for the forgiveness of sins for all peoples (Acts 2:39).

Thus as the church age began it was still centered in Israel and the disciples clearly hoped to bring their people to repentance in order to usher in the return of the Messiah and the dawn of the promised kingdom (Acts 3:19-20). In time the disciples began to understand the death and resurrection of the Messiah at the hands of their leaders was all within the eternal purposes of God (Acts 4:27-28). However when a great persecution began at the hands of Saul of Tarsus, they were forced to leave Jerusalem and begin to reach out to others just as Jesus had predicted.

Here began the great friction between Jew and Gentile that would come to dominate much of the New Testament. Initially the church was entirely Jewish but with time the number of Gentile believers grew and ultimately eclipsed the Jewish church which eventually became all but extinct after the revolts of the Jews in the second century A.D. This initial period of transition was not without its perils. The early church could easily have split along ethnic lines but the apostles and early leaders took great pains to keep the church united under the headship of Christ.

Acts chapter 10 is a particularly significant milestone for the development of the global church. Up to that point the church was almost uniformly Jewish in nature, until the Lord forced the issue by orchestrating a meeting of the Apostle Peter with the Roman centurion Cornelius. To the very end Peter was clearly hesitant and yet he could not deny the fact that the same Spirit that had baptized the Jewish believers in Pentecost had evidently baptized these Gentile believers too. Such was the consternation created by this incident that Peter is later called before a tribunal of Jewish elders in Jerusalem to give account of his actions. Finally they were forced to recognize that *"to the Gentiles also God has granted repentance that leads to life"* (Acts 11:18).

After Peter used the keys entrusted to him by Jesus to unlock the doors of the kingdom, the gospel began to spread like wildfire among the Gentiles. However it was still a very delicate subject for Jewish believers, many of whom could not stomach the new Gentile converts. Thus when Paul and Barnabas came back from their first missionary excursion among the Gentiles they were confronted with Jewish teachers insisting that all disciples of Jesus needed to submit to the rigors of the Mosaic

Law. Thus, the greatest challenge of the early church came to the fore: Do all believers of the Messiah need to keep the Law?

Such was the urgency of the question at hand that the early church convened the first church council to settle the matter. This was a critical moment in ecclesiastical history. The church could have easily splintered along ideological and ethnic fault lines. However, after great deliberation, the elders of the early church, all Jewish, concluded that only faith in Jesus Christ was necessary for salvation. They further noted that in order to help bridge the cultural divide and maintain peace between Jewish and Gentile believers, it would be advisable for the latter to abstain from eating non-kosher foods in the presence of their Jewish brethren (Acts 15).

Thus it was established that the church of Jesus Christ was neither Jewish nor anti-Jewish. While it rested firmly on the foundations of the Torah and the teachings of the Jewish prophets in accordance with the original covenant with Abraham, the church also welcomed all nations to benefit from the blessing of the Jewish Messiah. Even though it did not require its adherents to abide by the ceremonial laws of Israel it also did not belittle or scorn the rituals inherent to the original covenant for the Jewish believers who wanted to continue abiding by them.[10]

Later in writing his first letter to believers scattered throughout modern-day Turkey, the apostle Peter beautifully harmonizes many of the Old and New Covenant themes. In order to encourage persecuted believers he points them forward to the great inheritance and kingdom promised by the prophets. Then in chapter two he begins speaking of how God is building a new temple on the cornerstone of Jesus Christ with each of us being living stones in the building. Then he begins to use exclusively Old Testament imagery of priesthood and holy sacrifices to describe Jewish and Gentile believers. He then goes even further when he describes the church as *"a chosen race, a royal priesthood, a holy nation, a people for his own possession"* (1 Peter 2:9). This is remarkable!

Because of Peter's references here to the Old Testament some commentators assume he is writing exclusively to Jewish people. However in the following verses he makes it clear that he is speaking to the larger church which includes Gentiles when he says 'once you were not a people.' Evidently Peter has no qualms giving Old Covenant titles previously attributed exclusively to Israel to the New Covenant church. In his mind they are part of the same seamless continuum, all part of God's eternal plan. In doing so let's not make the mistake of thinking that he is replacing Israel with the church. Rather Peter, as a Jewish apostle, has come to recognize his fellow Gentile brothers and sisters as part of the greater family of God. It is not "either/or" but rather "both/and"...

This united theme is echoed in Paul's letters as well. In Ephesians 2 he notes that the largely Gentile church far from denigrating its Jewish heritage, should actually embrace it forming one new man. Instead of belittling the Jewish background of the faith, Paul welcomes all believers to draw near and be built up together on the foundation of the Jewish apostles and prophets. Thus Paul sees the church not as a compilation of rival nationalities but rather as one body clothed in the richness of various cultural and ethnic trappings (Ephesians 2:11-22).

Paul And The Jews

Throughout the book of Acts no one receives more scorn from the Jews than the Apostle Paul. Of course abandoning his earlier hard-line position against the church and becoming the champion of the Christian faith made him a marked man. However, despite all his run-ins with the Jewish community, his commitment to reach them with the gospel is unparalleled (Romans 9:1-5). From the beginning of his ministry to the last chapter of Acts we see him giving priority to the Jewish people in his gospel proclamation. Even though he was regularly maligned by them he was not embittered towards them but remained persistent in his preaching 'to the Jew first and then to the Gentile.' Why did he not give up on them?

In his epic gospel manifesto, the letter to the believers in Rome, Paul delivers a carefully thought through presentation of answers to the common objections related to his message. After decades of preaching the gospel across the Middle East, Paul knew by heart the questions his message would raise, many of which had to do with the relationship of the gospel to the Jews and their Law. In the letter to the Romans Paul was likely writing to a group of very cosmopolitan church fellowships composed of both Jews and Gentiles. From the content of the letter it is evident that they were having some serious debates surrounding some Jews' reservations related to certain foods. Thus Paul takes some time to clarify the relationship of the gospel to the Law and ultimately the choice of Israel and their future involvement in God's program.

In chapter one, after reaffirming his commitment to preaching the gospel to the Jews first as Jesus had, Paul goes on to paint the backdrop of the gospel, namely God's impending judgment in the face of gross human depravity. Now, the otherwise upright Jews would have been cheering Paul on this far, until he turns his guns on them in chapter 2. He stresses that just being a Jew does not absolve them, rather they are equally sinful, if anything because of their smug judgmental attitude. Then in chapter 3, he asks an important question: *'What is the advantage of being a Jew?'* We might be tempted to say that there is no advantage whatsoever, but Paul would disagree. He points out that the Jewish heritage brings with it unique prerogative to God's revelation.

Then he asks another pertinent question: Because the nation of Israel proved unworthy of God's calling, does their faithlessness nullify the faithfulness of God? Paul responds with an emphatic NO! If there was ever a place we would expect to find a clear denunciation of Israel and disqualification from future participation in God's redemptive program, this would be the place. In chapter 3, Paul goes on to emphasize that Jews and Gentiles are both equally sinful and separated from God and equally needful of one and the same redemption provided by Jesus Christ.

Later in Romans chapters 6-8, Paul touches on the role of the Law in our salvation. He makes it abundantly clear that New Covenant believers are not under the Mosaic Law because that legal system was designed to underscore our sinful nature not provide salvation. Paul says we have been released from the Law because we have died with Christ and are now bound to him. However, this does not mean that we are subject to no law, rather we are bound to the Law of the Spirit which operates within us. Thus Paul wants to be clear that when it comes to our salvation, amassing good works in accordance with the Law in no way gains us special favors with God. However, he is equally adamant in stating that believers in Jesus are not free to be a law unto themselves.

After concluding his treatise on the gospel, in chapters 9-11 of Romans the apostle Paul wants to walk us through the role of Israel in redemptive history. He does this because a proper understanding of Israel's place in God's economy is essential to a full grasp of the gospel. These chapters provide us with the most compelling answers with regards to our original question of what we as followers in Jesus should believe about ethnic Israel.

The apostle Paul starts by stating in unequivocal terms his great love for Israel and his desire for their salvation. He then speaks to their unique status as the chosen people of God. But then comes the question: Has God's plan failed on account of Jewish rejection of Christ? He had promised to make them a blessing to all nations, but as Paul writes this his people the Jews had been effectively cursed for their refusal to accept Jesus as the promised Messiah.

Paul begins his answer with the cryptic statement: *"For not all who are descended from Israel belong to Israel, and not all are children of Abraham because they are his offspring"* (9:6-7) What does he mean? He goes on to point out that God's choice of the nation of Israel was not based on their biological heritage (not Ishmael but Isaac) or their moral uprightness (not Esau but Jacob). Rather, the election of Israel was a unilateral decision based on God's sovereign choice and his gracious promise to Abraham.

After a brief discussion on God's right to act sovereignly in his choices, Paul points out that God chose to endure the rebellion of the Jewish people knowing that it would ultimately serve to draw the nations to himself. Then the apostle quotes from several Old Testament passages that speak to the salvation of the Gentiles as well as to the salvation of only a remnant of Israel. Notice he doesn't say that the Gentile believers have replaced Israel in God's program, rather he notes that they are saved by faith while the Jews were largely rejected for the lack thereof. However he still has hope for the remnant of his people Israel.

At the outset of Romans 10, Paul reiterates his heart's desire and constant prayer for the salvation of his people Israel. He vouches for their religious zeal but points out their misguided faith in their own ability to attain righteousness through the Law rather than accepting the gift of salvation through Jesus Christ. All along Paul has made it abundantly clear that salvation for Jews and Gentiles has only ever been available through faith. Consequently, faith comes from hearing the gospel. But if the Jews failed to pass the message along to the nations, how will they be saved?

The question of the unreached has often posed a real challenge to believers, namely, how will God judge those who never had a chance to respond to the gospel of Jesus Christ? Earlier in Romans Paul pointed out that while the Jews will be judged by their knowledge of God's laws, Gentiles will be judged by the moral laws engraved on their conscience (Romans 2:12-16). In Romans 10, Paul goes a step further pointing out that even though the Jews largely failed to promulgate the gospel to the nations, the message has still echoed across the planet through God's general revelation in creation (Romans 10:18).

Thus we can be certain that anyone who has ever genuinely desired to know the Lord has been found by him.[11]

The next verse, however, introduces the all-important subject of 'jealousy.' Paul quotes from the Torah where Moses predicts the disobedience of Israel but also God's choice of the Gentiles to bring them to jealousy (Deuteronomy 32:21). Paul believes that as more and more of the Gentiles flock to the Jewish Messiah this will ultimately have a cumulative effect on Israel forcing them to comes to terms with their rejection of Yeshua. Thus Paul is hopeful that Gentile believers will ultimately serve as the necessary catalyst for his people Israel's final salvation.

Jealousy Leading To Repentance

Before moving on to Romans 11, we need to fill in the Biblical background to Paul's understanding of 'holy jealousy.' The prophetic writings are full of God's judgments directed at Israel for her unfaithfulness. The Lord also establishes his sovereignty over the nations by leveling his judgment on them as well. In one such indictment of Egypt in Isaiah 19, we are suddenly transported to a yet future time when the enemy nations of the Middle East come to know the Lord and in turn draw Israel back to God. All this takes place in relation to the great 'Highway' theme.

The word here speaks of a 'higher' way (Hb: Mesillah), a new kind of transcontinental link that transcends millennia of regional strife and ethnic animosity. It all starts with Egypt, the first great oppressor of Israel. Isaiah predicts a great revival in the land of the Nile. However this great renewal will come at a great cost: 'striking but healing.' Furthermore, this national redemption will be worked out practically in an unparalleled spiritual bond with their historical nemesis Assyria to the north, all of which takes place along the 'highway.'

In that day there will be a highway from Egypt to Assyria, and

> *Assyria will come into Egypt, and Egypt into Assyria, and the Egyptians will worship with the Assyrians. In that day Israel will be the third with Egypt and Assyria, a blessing in the midst of the earth, whom the LORD of hosts has blessed, saying, "Blessed be Egypt my people, and Assyria the work of my hands, and Israel my inheritance'* (Isaiah 19:23-25).

To date this highway prophecy has not been fulfilled. Travel by land between these troubled countries today is impossible but a literal highway may indeed be built in the millennial reign of Christ. However, there seems to be a 'higher' meaning here pointing to a spiritual alliance between these historic rivals. The prophecy indicates that the spiritual revival and subsequent union of Egypt and Assyria will ultimately serve to draw Israel into a great spiritual camaraderie and by doing so will help fulfill its ultimate purpose of being a blessing to the nations. Sadly Israel has largely been a source of much consternation and even a curse in the Middle East to date, but this will surely change. Ironically, according to Isaiah, it will be the revival in its pagan neighbors to the south and the north that will ultimately serve to spark Israel's repentance and restoration.

Notice also it is the spiritual bond around God's truth that creates unprecedented unity and peace in these rival nations, not some political maneuver. We have all witnessed seemingly endless rounds of diplomatic efforts to bring peace to the Holy Land over the last century, but all have failed miserably. However in Isaiah 19 we see the power of prayer and worship at work. Ultimately these nations that were once at odds now receive a new identity because of their unprecedented unity around God's purposes.

On a personal note I have had the privilege of visiting the land of Israel on several occasions. Most of these visits have been in conjunction with a conference for pastors from around the Middle East. I have had the joy of translating for the Turkish delegation as they engage with other ministers from across this troubled region sharing stories of God's faithfulness and praying towards a revival in the land. On one of these trips we were approached by an Israeli news agency asking for an interview. They were deeply stirred when they heard that Turkish, Kurdish, Arab, Persian and Jewish believers in Yeshua were gathering in Jerusalem for worship and prayer. Normally people from these diverse ethnic backgrounds should be at each others' throats, but instead here we were embracing and crying out together for God's mercy to be poured out on the Middle East. It was a practical reminder to us all how the united body of Christ can serve as a catalyst for 'holy jealousy' to the Jewish nation in particular.

The fact that Israel will undergo a miraculous restoration in the end times is echoed throughout the prophets. Earlier Isaiah spoke of the Jewish people returning to their land from the four corners of the earth and becoming a spiritual magnet to Gentile believers worldwide in the last days (Isaiah 11, 14:1-2). He further speaks of the 'highway of holiness' by which the Jews will return and be established in the promised land (Isaiah 35, 49:22-23, 56:6-7). These prophecies seem to relate directly to the return of the Jewish people to their historic land in the 20th century after millennia of suffering in exile. However the fullness of these promises await a spiritual revival in the land of Israel.

The prophet Ezekiel painted a portrait of this final restoration of the nation of Israel in his famous vision of the valley of dry bones (Ezekiel 37). However, in the preceding chapter the Lord lays the foundation for this by prophesying the yet future regathering of the Jewish people and their national 'cleansing' from their spiritual filthiness.

I will take you from the nations and gather you from all the countries and bring you into your own land. I will sprinkle clean water on you, and you shall be clean from all your uncleannesses, and from all your idols I will cleanse you. And I will give you a new heart, and a new spirit I will put within you. And I will remove the heart of stone from your flesh and give you a heart of flesh. And I will put my Spirit within you, and cause you to walk in my statutes and be careful to obey my rules. You shall dwell in the land that I gave to your fathers, and you shall be my people, and I will be your God. And I will deliver you from all your uncleannesses (Ezekiel 36:24-29b).

Clearly the ultimate salvation and restoration of Israel is contingent on their spiritual regeneration. The language used here is clearly reminiscent of the New Covenant promises recorded by the prophet Jeremiah (31:31-34). This new order was inaugurated by Jesus himself even as he became the perfect sacrifice once for all (Hebrews 10:10). In short the promised salvation of Israel will ultimately become a reality when in the midst of national repentance they receive divine revelation leading them to accept Yeshua as their awaited Messiah.

Finally, the prophet Zechariah gives us in all likelihood the most detailed description of the yet future restoration of Israel based on their national repentance. In the context of the last days' military conflagration surrounding Jerusalem, the prophet foretells a time of great national mourning:

And I will pour out on the house of David and the inhabitants of Jerusalem a spirit of grace and pleas for mercy, so that, when they look on me, on him whom they have pierced, they shall mourn for him, as one mourns for an only child, and weep bitterly over him, as one weeps over a firstborn (Zechariah 12:10).

The subject of Israel's mourning is clearly a new-found recognition of the Messiah, 'the one they have pierced.' Even as Jerusalem is about to be overwhelmed by an international army gathered for the battle of armageddon, the nation of Israel finally comes to terms with their colossal error in having crucified their promised King. Establishing this important Biblical context is essential to understanding what Paul means in Romans 11, when he says that *'all Israel will be saved.'*

The Olive Tree

In Romans 11, Paul has already ascertained God's choice of Israel in the past and their present state of rebellion. Now he turns his attention to their future: Has God rejected his people Israel? Again Paul responds with an emphatic NO! First he points to the simple fact that he as a Jew is clearly a part of God's ongoing redemptive program. Secondly he takes us back to the example of Elijah when he imagined that there were no other faithful believers left aside from himself. At that time God revealed to him that he had preserved a 'remnant' unto himself. Likewise, Paul stresses that although most of the nation of Israel had succumbed to spiritual blindness on account of their rejection of the Messiah, God had indeed still saved some and would in fact spare a remnant.

As we noted earlier, the early church was almost exclusively Jewish until God forced them to reach out to the nations. Soon the number of Gentile believers by far surpassed the number of Jewish believers. Over the last two millennia since the destruction of the temple and the subsequent dispersion of Israel, there has never been a national revival among the Jewish people. Quite the contrary, because of the persecution they often suffered at the hands of Christians, they have been wary of the gospel of Jesus. However, that is not to say that there have been no believers from Jewry. On the contrary, as Paul notes, there has always been a remnant. Today, although relatively few, the number of Jewish believers in Israel and abroad is steadily growing.

Clearly the Jewish people have been hardened against the gospel, but does that mean they will never recover? Paul again responds emphatically: NO! He insists that this was in fact God's plan all along. Namely, just as by the Jew's transgression the gospel has gone to the Gentiles, by the latter's salvation Israel will be made jealous so as to return to the Messiah. Thus, he looks forward to the promised 'fullness', namely when Jews and Gentiles are all brought together under the headship of Christ.

Next, the great apostle addresses the Gentiles in particular, urging them not to despise their Jewish brethren but to love them as he does and to seek to make them 'jealous' regarding Yeshua. Sadly, this urgent call has gone unheeded far too long, with Christians down through the centuries more than often maligning Israel and persecuting the Jews. Further attempts, using theological constructs to sideline and ultimately disenfranchise Israel by claiming the church has replaced her in God's eternal purposes, has likewise exacerbated this divide. It is time we harken to Paul's plea and learn to sacrificially love Israel for God's sake and welcome them back to center stage in God's story of redemption.

Paul then appeals to the olive tree parable in order to explain the correlation between Israel and the new Gentile believers. The cultivated olive tree clearly represents the nation of Israel rooted in the 'seed' covenant God made with Abraham (Jeremiah 11:16). Later while some of the natural branches, namely the Jewish people, were cut off because of disobedience, other wild olive branches, namely Gentiles, were grafted onto the tree. In speaking to Gentile believers Paul's point is that they have no right to be puffed up and judgmental of their Jewish counterparts because they are ultimately held up by Jewish roots. The apostle goes further to predict that one day the original Jewish branches will again be grafted onto the olive tree.

It is important to note here that Paul does not see the original olive tree chopped down and replaced with a new tree. Rather he sees that it has been severely pruned for lack of fruit, just as Jesus predicted (John 15). He further sees Gentile believers as being accommodated by the original root structure. Elsewhere Paul points out that those who share the faith of Abraham, both Jews and Gentiles, are all partakers of that original covenant (Galatians 3). Ultimately God's desire is not to perpetuate a Church vs Israel rivalry but to merge believers of all backgrounds into one new family (Ephesians 3:1-13).

That being said, Paul wants to make certain that we don't make the mistake of assuming that God is finished with ethnic Israel. The fact that the olive tree today is overwhelmingly Gentile in appearance does not negate God's original purposes:

> *Lest you be wise in your own sight, I do not want you to be unaware of this mystery, brothers: a partial hardening has come upon Israel, until the fullness of the Gentiles has come in.* **And in this way all Israel will be saved,** *as it is written, "The Deliverer will come from Zion, he will banish ungodliness from Jacob"; "and this will be my covenant with them when I take away their sins." As regards the gospel, they are enemies for your sake. But as regards election, they are beloved for the sake of their forefathers. For the gifts and the calling of God are irrevocable* (Romans 11:25-29).

Although we live in a time when God's people are largely made up of Gentiles, Paul is emphatic that before the end comes, the Jewish people will also respond en masse to the gospel. In fact he believes that 'all Israel' will be saved. That is clearly a controversial statement. However if we pay attention to the prophetic reference he cites we can understand his reasoning.

Paul quotes from Isaiah 59, which speaks of a day when God himself will accomplish redemption for his people. It describes the Lord coming to Zion as a warrior to fight for his people and establish his kingdom. This he does in the context of the established New Covenant. Paul's point is quite straight-forward, namely, the Lord Jesus Christ is slated to return to Jerusalem. However, for him to be able to return, the Jewish people need to repent and welcome him back as their rightful king (Matthew 23:37-39). Thus the salvation of Israel is contingent on their national repentance, described earlier by the prophets, which will finally clear the way for the Lord's return to earth.

The very fact that Jesus is returning to Jerusalem, not Paris or New York, reminds us of the unique role Israel plays in history and will continue to play in the unfolding of God's eternal purposes. To believe that these plans have been altered is to believe that God did not know what he was doing from the beginning. On a practical note, in sharing the gospel with Muslims one of their common arguments is that just as the New Testament replaced the Old Testament, so the Quran replaces the Bible. This false deduction is based on the assumption that the gospel of Jesus Christ has done away with its precedent in the Jewish covenants. Thus, it is imperative in our gospel presentation to emphasize our acceptance of both the Old and New Covenants but also to stress that we believe in one plan of salvation represented in the whole counsel of God from Genesis to Revelation.

Going back to Paul's dissertation on Israel, he wraps up his arguments by stressing that the original choice, later rejection and final redemption of the Jewish people was all the fruit of God's great wisdom from eternity past (Romans 11:33-36). So it is that God's calling of Israel is indeed irrevocable, just as Israel is irreplaceable in the divine drama. This is why the prophets and apostles urge us to love the Jewish people and take pains to help them see 'the one they have pierced.' In the end, regardless of our attitude towards the Jewish people, the Scriptures are clear of how God feels about them.

> But Zion said, "The LORD has forsaken me; my Lord has forgotten me." "Can a woman forget her nursing child, that she should have no compassion on the son of her womb? Even these may forget, yet I will not forget you. Behold, I have engraved you on the palms of my hands; your walls are continually before me. (Isaiah 49:14-16).

Conclusion

It is no secret that Israel has played and will continue

to play a monumental role in Christian history and theology. Not only is Christendom built on the foundation of the Old Covenant, we also owe our Scriptures to the Jewish people. These same texts when interpreted forthrightly give us every reason to believe that God is not finished with Israel, if anything because he is a covenant God who keeps his promises. This fact alone should be a great source of comfort to all believers regardless of their ethnic background.

Although Jesus' interactions with the Jewish leaders ended with him being crucified and his resurrection being called a sham, the Lord remained committed to loving and serving his people. This was further evidenced by his followers investing themselves fully in the church of Jerusalem. They clearly did not see themselves as a new sect or off-shoot of Judaism but rather as the natural outgrowth and fulfillment of the long cherished prophecies entrusted to Israel. Thus they continued to meet in the temple and worship in accordance with Jewish laws until they were later forced to leave Jerusalem under the threat of death.

In a similar way Paul, despite being oft maligned by Judaizers, worked tirelessly for the salvation of his people, being willing to be 'accursed and cut off from Christ for their sake' if that would somehow guarantee their redemption. Ultimately he came to believe that his people's restoration would only be possible if Gentile believers in turn spurred the Jews on to jealousy. It is further clear from many Old Testament passages that Israel's repentance and ultimate restoration is the linchpin for the return of Christ and the fulfillment of his kingdom. Thus we do well to 'pray for the peace of Jerusalem.'

Finally we do well to take stock of Jesus' prophetic words with regard to the final state of his 'flock.'

> I am the good shepherd. I know my own and my own know me, just as the Father knows me and I know the Father; and I lay down my life for the sheep. And I have other sheep that are not of this fold. I must bring them also, and they will listen

to my voice. So there will be one flock, one shepherd (John 10:14-16).

In this parable Jesus draws on rich Old Testament imagery linking him to God the great Shepherd of Israel (Psalm 23; Ecclesiastes 12:11), as well as to the Messiah who will regather the Jewish nation into one flock (Ezekiel 34:11-24; Zechariah 11:7-14). He is clearly referring to the Jewish nation as his flock, but then he also speaks of 'other sheep that are not of this fold,' an obvious reference to future Gentile believers. Notice, that he is not making a new pen for them, but rather bringing them into one and the same fold. His stated purpose is as clear as day: **'So there will be one flock,** *one shepherd'* (See also: Isaiah 56:6-7).

Dispensationalists, who have historically defended the continued place of Israel in God's program, have also taught a very strict and rigid distinction between Israel and the church. Reformed theologians on the other hand, have often made the mistake of completely excluding Israel from God's future plans and seeing all of God's purposes enshrined in the church. However a more nuanced and Biblically balanced position would have us retain Israel as the locus of God's purposes even as we see her and the church ultimately merge into one people, namely the household of God (Ephesians 2:19).

While maintaining a rigid distinction between Israel and the church makes it easier to navigate questions about Gentile believers' commitment to the Law, it ultimately creates an unbiblical dichotomy in which God deals differently with two separate entities. The 'Covenant' position, which erases all the distinctions and effectively supplants historic Israel with the church, ultimately forces them to have to allegorize many of the Old Testament promises made to the nation of Israel. In the end, both interpretive frameworks are found wanting.

Is it possible to find a middle ground? I believe so. Instead of taking sides, we do best to avoid extreme and reactionary positions and benefit from the strong suit of each.

We can affirm the ongoing unique place of ethnic Israel in God's eschatological program even as we see the church being instrumental in bringing the Jewish people to jealousy so that both can ultimately be united in the kingdom of Christ. For the time being, the church is leading the charge in calling all nations, including Israel, back to God, and in this way we are God's chosen people. However we wouldn't dare to claim we are replacing God's specific promises to ethnic Israel as these have yet to be fulfilled in the last days.

4. THE SIGNS

Since I was a child I've always loved poring over maps. Having lived now on four different continents and traveling as I often do, I find maps to be invaluable. For some people maps may be boring, especially if they can't make any sense of the unique cartographical signs and symbols. But I like looking over a map before going to a new location in order to become familiar with the landscape and historic landmarks of the place I will be visiting. Even if I don't know exactly what the place will look like I can almost begin to visualize it from the signs on the map. More importantly, when I do get there I already have a sense of where I am and I'm not easily disoriented.

Prophecy in the Bible is much like a map of the future. It gives us a general outline with some specific signs and symbols that will help us navigate those troubled waters when we actually get there. Trying to make sense of the details and getting everything charted out in advance can sometimes be frustrating if not impossible because we don't have all the information we would like to have. This is because by design prophecy forces us to step out in faith. We have enough information to know we can trust God's wisdom but not enough that we can we smug in our own interpretations.

In a way it's like giving directions to someone. In the Middle East whenever you need help you can always count on people to give you directions. Even if they have no clue of the place you are asking they will never confess to not knowing. In fact, I'm convinced that the word "I don't know" is missing from the Turkish vocabulary, as they always have an opinion about everything. However suppose you do find someone who knows the place you are asking, the directions will go something like this: *'My friend, just walk down this street for a ways, let's say 200-300 meters, then you will see a big red door on your left. Turn left there and go straight for a bit. You will come to a green cafe, say hi to the owner for me, but keep going and then you will come to an old blue bus parked on the sidewalk on your right, turn right there. After a few meters, maybe a hundred meters, I'm not sure, you will see a big yellow sign with some black letters on your right, I can't remember what it says, but you cannot miss it. Your destination is around the corner from there. You got it, right?'*

Now as nerve-racking as this experience might be for a westerner, he will find that if he does follow the ad hoc signs, vague though they may be, he will sooner or later reach his destination. However he will only recognize those clues as he is moving forward in faith. In a similar way God's Word gives us quite a number of specific signs regarding the end times but they will only make sense to believers that are following the clues as they approach the final destination. Thus we cannot hope to make absolute sense of all the details in advance, the best we can do is know the sequence of the signs so that when we get there we will easily recognize them and know what to expect.

The prophets of the Old Testament faced a similar dilemma. The apostle Peter when writing to the believers scattered across the Middle East praises them for truly loving the Lord even though they have not seen him. They were confident of Christ's return even though they were forced to wait patiently. Then he points to the prophet's experience as an example for believers in the church age:

> *Concerning this salvation, the prophets who prophesied about the grace that was to be yours searched and inquired carefully, inquiring what person or time the Spirit of Christ in them was indicating when he predicted the sufferings of Christ*

and the subsequent glories. It was revealed to them that they were serving not themselves but you, in the things that have now been announced to you through those who preached the good news to you by the Holy Spirit sent from heaven, things into which angels long to look (1 Peter 1:10-12).

The prophets really did their homework. And yet, even though they tried their hardest to make sense of all the conflicting information they were receiving about the promised Messiah, in the end they had to accept that their task was simply to draw the map for future generations (See: Daniel 12:8-10; Hebrews 11:39-40). In our case however, we may in fact be that generation that steps into that period of history so carefully charted out long ago by God's servants. Thus we do well to pay attention to the details in God's map of the future, the Bible.

Now as we delve into the many signs of the end times we would not presume to know exactly how it will all go down. Rather, based on the Scriptures we want to establish the main landmarks and chart a course on a map as it were, so that as the time approaches we will not miss the signs. You might be surprised to know that many other religions, including Islam, also have a list of signs of the end. While many of these like the rise of a red moon or micro-chip implants have become urban myths, we do well to take stock of the Biblical warnings in this regard.

Rejection And Restoration

Towards the end of Christ's ministry on earth, after being repeatedly rejected by the Jewish leaders, Jesus began to speak openly about his second coming. Luke records these instances in great detail. Using first the example of a master and his servants Jesus urged his disciples to be ever ready for his return and diligent in their work. Then he chided the Jews for being so good at predicting the next day's weather based on the clouds but not being able to recognize the sings of prophetic events that were transpiring before their eyes (Luke 12:35-56).

Later Jesus told them outright that soon he would no longer be among them. Besides predicting his upcoming sufferings in Jerusalem, he also spoke to the future conditions of the earth before his second coming. He likened the final moral condition of the world to the times of Noah and Lot. At that time, mankind had become so shamelessly depraved that God was compelled to destroy them wholesale. And yet, even on those occasions, God was able to deliver a few and restore a remnant to himself (Luke 17:22-37).

Finally, by entering Jerusalem in fulfillment of the prophecy of Zechariah, Jesus gave the Jewish people one last chance to recognize him. However upon the Jewish ruling establishment's utter rejection and subsequent challenge of his spiritual authority, Jesus laid out his final indictment of Israel. Chapter 23 of Matthew is a resounding condemnation of the Jewish religious leadership in Jesus' day. His scathing rebuke set up his final verdict to be outlined in chapter 24. However just before that he again expressed his heart-felt grief for their spiritual blindness:

> "O Jerusalem, Jerusalem, the city that kills the prophets and stones those who are sent to it! How often would I have gathered your children together as a hen gathers her brood under her wings, and you were not willing! See, your house is left to you desolate. For I tell you, you will not see me again, until you say, 'Blessed is he who comes in the name of the Lord" (Matthew 23:37-39).

After lamenting their great sin Jesus spoke to the upcoming destruction of the temple as a judgment for their unwillingness to recognize him as their Messiah. Then he gave one the most significant signs of the second coming. He stated that the Jewish people would see him only when they say, "Blessed is he who comes in the name of the Lord.' This phrase always mystified me until I learned that to this day Jews use a shortened form of this phrase (Hb: Baruk haba) to welcome people. In formal settings they still use a phrase almost identical to the longer version that Jesus alluded to. In short, Jesus was saying that he would not return until his people, ethnic Jews, welcomed him back.

It is also important to note that Jesus' words here allude to Psalm 118 where we also read the famous verse of the stone the builders rejected.[12] This prophetic passage highlights the fact that since Israel rejected the Lord's chosen one, God would reject the Jews and their temple and build another temple, a spiritual one, upon the cornerstone of the Messiah (Ephesians 2:20-21; 1 Peter 2:4-9). Interestingly the cry of the people on Christ's triumphal entry, Hosanna (Lord, save us!), also harkens to this psalm (verse 25). Sadly, even though the people wanted Jesus to be their Savior, the leaders outright refused to acknowledge him as such and by condemning him to death, they likewise condemned the whole nation to spiritual exile. However, none of this was a surprise as the prophets predicted this from the outset. So it is that Jesus' triumphal return to establish his kingdom is contingent on the repentance of Israel.

This should not surprise us because Jesus came as the promised Messiah of Israel. God had made an unconditional covenant with Abraham, that he would bless his descendants and make them a blessing to all nations. He followed this up with a number of other covenants and myriads of promises in the Old Testament directed to the nation of Israel. We saw earlier that God's calling is irrevocable and that he promised to save Israel in the end. Here in Matthew, we see that indeed the restoration of Israel to God's purposes, with them finally acknowledging Yeshua as Messiah, will clear the way for his glorious return and the final establishment of his kingdom on earth.

How exactly this will happen we do not know. To date Jews have proven very resistant to the gospel, however, the very fact that they still exist, after having survived multiple attempts of annihilation over the past 2000 years, is powerful testimony of God's commitment to his ongoing purposes for Israel. Furthermore, since the establishment of the modern state of Israel in 1948, their resilience in a sea of Muslim countries, ever plotting their extermination, is further evidence of God's hand of protection over them. Today, a growing number of Messianic congregations in the land of Israel are laboring and praying towards this promised restoration.

The prophet Zechariah tells us that when the nation of Israel does finally come to terms with their colossal failure to recognize Yeshua the Messiah, they will undergo a time of deep mourning that will lead to spiritual cleansing and full restoration (Zechariah 12:10-14). The book of Revelation also hints at a renewed role for the Jewish people in a global revival during the great tribulation. The 144,000 elect are clearly of Jewish origin and they are described as a unique group of Jesus followers dedicated to the cause of the gospel (Revelation 7:1-8, 14:1-5). Their global ministry will likely be greatly influenced by the powerful witness of two Jewish prophets stationed at the temple in Jerusalem at that time (Revelation 11). More will be said about these in a later chapter.

A lesson from Jewish history can be helpful here. When the Jewish people returned from their first exile after the destruction of Solomon's temple, the promised restoration took some time to unfold. The first group of exiles returned around 538 B.C. by edict of King Cyrus of Persia. They were tasked with rebuilding the temple. However, after starting out strong they stalled out for 20 years and did not continue until God used the prophets Haggai and Zechariah to spur them on in finishing the construction of the temple. However at this time the city was still in ruins and the people's hearts far from God. It wasn't until some 80 years after the end of the exile (458 B.C.) that God sent Ezra and later Nehemiah to call the people of Israel to repent and participate in the final rebuilding of the city of Jerusalem.

In a similar way I suspect the final restoration of Israel will not take place overnight. For now they have returned to their land from exile, which was an essential first step, but their hearts are still far from God. The Bible indicates that sometime before the end a temple will be rebuilt in Jerusalem which will subsequently be desecrated by the antichrist (2 Thessalonians 2:4). More importantly however, during that final time of great distress, the hearts of God's people Israel will somehow be turned back to God. As we saw earlier the Gentile believers are called upon to play a crucial role in this by arousing the Jewish people to holy jealousy.

The Olivet Discourse

After highlighting the first obstacle to Christ's return and kingdom, namely ongoing Jewish rejection of the Messiah, chapter 24 of Matthew provides us with the most detailed discussion of the signs of the latter times. Sadly, traditional dispensationalists have undermined the crucial message of this chapter claiming it is not for the church, as she will be raptured prior to this, but rather for the nation of Israel as it endures the great tribulation. If that were the case why does the apostle Paul discuss these same events in writing to a New Testament church? (1 Thessalonians 5; 1 Thessalonians 2). We will leave discussion of the rapture to a later chapter but for now let it suffice to say that we ignore these warnings at our own peril.

Conversely, reformed theologians, many of whom do not see a future role for Israel or even a millennial kingdom, find themselves forced to interpret these passages allegorically or historically. Some teach that Jesus was only predicting the imminent destruction of the temple as the hands of the Romans, thus negating any yet future fulfillment. While there is certainly a correlation to the events of 70 A.D., the fact that Jesus has not yet returned, as the latter part of the chapter indicates, clearly points us to some yet future fulfillment as well. Here is another case of 'both/and' rather than 'either/or.' Before getting into the details let's take a moment to just read the passage in its entirety and allow it to speak for itself:

Jesus left the temple and was going away, when his disciples came to point out to him the buildings of the temple. But he answered them, "You see all these, do you not? Truly, I say to you, there will not be left here one stone upon another that will not be thrown down." As he sat on the Mount of Olives, the disciples came to him privately, saying, "Tell us, when will these things be, and what will be the sign of your coming and of the end of the age?" And Jesus answered them, "See that no one leads you astray. For many will come in my name, saying, 'I am the Christ,' and they will lead many astray. And you will hear of wars and rumors of wars. See that you are not alarmed, for this must take place, but the end is not yet. For nation will rise against nation, and kingdom against kingdom, and there will be famines and earthquakes in various places. All these are but the beginning of the birth pains. "Then they will deliver you up to tribulation and put you to death, and you will be hated by all nations for my name's sake. And then many will fall away and betray one another and hate one another. And many false prophets will arise and lead many astray. And because lawlessness will be increased, the love of many will grow cold. But the one who endures to the end will be saved. And this gospel of the kingdom will be proclaimed throughout the whole world as a testimony to all nations, and then the end will come. "So when you see the abomination of desolation spoken of by the prophet Daniel, standing in the holy place (let the reader understand), then let those who are in Judea flee to the mountains. Let the one who is on the housetop not go down to take what is in his house, and let the one who is in the field not turn back to take his cloak. And alas for women who are pregnant and for those who are nursing infants in those days! Pray that your flight may not be in winter or on a Sabbath. For then there will be great tribulation, such as has not been from the beginning of the world until now, no, and never will be. And if those days had not been cut short, no human being would be saved. But for the sake of the elect those days will be cut short. Then if anyone says to you, 'Look, here is the Christ!' or 'There he is!' do not believe it. For false christs and false prophets will arise and perform great signs and wonders, so as to lead astray, if possible, even the elect. See, I have told you beforehand. So, if they say to you, 'Look, he is in the wilderness,' do not go out. If they say, 'Look, he is in the inner rooms,' do not believe it. For as the lightning comes from the east and shines as far as the west, so will be the coming of the Son of Man. Wherever the corpse is, there the vultures will gather. "Immediately after the tribulation of those days the sun will be darkened, and the moon will not give its light, and the stars will fall from heaven, and the powers of the heavens will be shaken. Then will appear in heaven the sign of the Son of Man, and then all the tribes of the earth will mourn, and they will see the Son of Man coming on the clouds of heaven with power and great glory. And he will send out his angels with a loud trumpet call, and they will gather his elect from the four winds, from one end of heaven to the other (Matthew 24:1-31).

Setting the context of this all-important passage is essential to its interpretation. On the heels of his devastating indictment of the Jewish nation in the previous chapter, Jesus took his disciples and walked out of Jerusalem. As they made their way up the hillside opposite the temple, towards Bethany where they were staying just beyond the crest of the Mount of Olives, a breath-taking panoramic view of Jerusalem with the temple mount in the foreground unfolded behind them. Looking back the disciples couldn't help but admire the great Jewish temple restored by Herod the Great, gilded with gold and bustling with Passover pilgrims from all over the diaspora. Jesus however shocked them when he went on to prophecy the utter destruction of the pride and joy of Israel. In fact he said a total demolition was in store for the temple, the symbol of God's presence in the land.

The disciples responded by asking two questions which they likely assumed were contemporaneous: *"Tell us, when will these things be, and what will be the sign of your coming and of the end of the age?"* They were asking about the timing of the destruction of the temple assuming that Christ would come and establish his kingdom at that time. However, in the following verses it becomes evident that Jesus is actually speaking of two different events separated by thousands of years but ultimately related as they both touch on the destruction of the temple. In order to unravel this enigmatic passage we need to gain a better understanding of the prophetic phenomena known as 'dual fulfillment.'

Dual Fulfillment

Also known as 'double reference' or 'multiple fulfillment', this hermeneutical principle unique to the Bible helps us makes sense of passages in Scripture that have more than one obvious reference or target.[13] Of course, the general rule of thumb for sound Biblical interpretation is that every verse has one meaning but many applications. However, it is also an established fact that events in the Old Testament will often find secondary meaning and ultimate fulfillment in the New Testament (Hebrews 10:1). Dispensationalists have traditionally tried to steer clear of any 'allegorical' type of interpretation, and yet the Biblical authors themselves at times stress layers of meaning, including spiritual and allegorical meanings, in the text (Galatians 4:21-31; Hebrews 7). This again is an example where we should pursue an inclusive 'both/and' form of interpretation rather than an exclusive 'either/or' format.

There are numerous forms of dual fulfillment in the Scriptures. Although some are easier to spot than others, they are all ultimately rooted in a sound and straightforward interpretation of the text. The most common is what is called a 'type', namely a person or event that foreshadows something or someone in the future. These are usually portraits that prefigure the Lord Jesus Christ. Examples of these include the lives of Melchizedek, Isaac, Joseph, Moses and David which in many unique ways 'typify' or foreshadowed the life of Christ. Likewise, inanimate structures like the tabernacle or religious feasts like the Passover also prefigured the life and ministry of Jesus. Thus, these were real people, places and events that took place in history and yet had a greater purpose in pointing us to Christ.

When it comes to prophecy it is important to remember that the prophets were not exclusively speaking of things yet future. In fact the majority of their ministry was focused on calling the people of their time to repentance. Thus their focus was more than often on their local and immediate context. Then there are those exceptional passages where they begin speaking to events yet future, often as a means of encouraging their people with regard to God's faithfulness. Thus in the prophetic writings there is often a puzzling interchange in which the authors move seamlessly from present to future events and between more than one yet future event (See: Isaiah 61:1-3; Zechariah 9:9-10; Malachi 3:1-4). Because of this it is often hard to decipher if they are referring to something present or future or to both.

A classic example of this is the covenant made with David in 2 Samuel 7. God promised to bless the king's descendants and perpetuate his kingdom. In the immediate context there is a clear reference to David's son Solomon who would build the temple. However, it is also clear that there is a greater 'Son' in mind whose reign would last forever, namely the Messiah. Many passages in the Old Testament allude to this greater Son (Psalm 2; Isaiah 9:7) as do many passages in the New Testament (Luke 1:32-33). Thus the Davidic Covenant begins to find its fulfillment immediately in the life of Solomon but it awaits its ultimate fulfillment in the millennial reign of Christ.

Another dual reference can be observed in the gospels when Matthew claims that the virgin birth of Jesus is a fulfillment of the 'Immanuel' prophecy of Isaiah 7. This is puzzling to many who upon reading the relevant passage in the

Old Testament find that the 'Immanuel' prophesied there seems to refer some remarkable child whose birth would serve as a sign to King Ahaz of God's faithfulness. However if we continue to read Isaiah's text we promptly come upon another 'child' to be born, who would quite literally be 'Immanuel', that is 'God with us' (Isaiah 9:6). The gospel writer, Matthew, seeing this bigger picture, has no qualms about connecting Jesus to the greater Immanuel prophecy because Christ is the culmination of God's promises.

Examples of this type of dual fulfillment or double reference in prophetic texts abound (Genesis 22:18; Hosea 11:1; Joel 2:28-32). However understanding the reasoning behind this phenomena in prophecy is important. The Scriptures often warned of false prophets who would deceive God's people. Manipulating God's message was a serious crime in Israel punishable by death. In the Torah the Israelites ask a pertinent question: *'How may we know the word that the LORD has not spoken?'* To which God responds: *When a prophet speaks in the name of the LORD, if the word does not come to pass or come true, that is a word that the LORD has not spoken; the prophet has spoken it presumptuously. You need not be afraid of him'* (Deuteronomy 18:22). Thus, in order to be certain that a person truly spoke for God, he needed to be able to predict with absolute accuracy something in the near future that would serve as his license to prophecy.

This was an important rite of passage for Biblical prophets because otherwise anyone could begin predicting events in the future and never live to be held accountable for his words. However, if they made a verifiable short-term prediction, this would serve as their endorsement from God. The prophet Jeremiah found himself in just such a predicament when Hananiah prophesied the opposite of what God had spoken before through the prophet. In order to show that Hananiah was an impostor, Jeremiah gave a very clear sign saying, *'This year you shall die, because you have uttered rebellion against the LORD.'* In that same year, in the seventh month, the false prophet

Hananiah died. (Jeremiah 28:16-17). Thus the prophet Jeremiah was vindicated, furthermore, the people now had every reason to believe that what he had predicted about the destruction of the temple, the exile and the return to the land, would also come to pass.

It is this dual fulfillment pattern established in the Old Testament that serves as the backdrop for Jesus' predictions of the destruction of the second temple. Especially in the parallel passage in Luke, it is quite evident that Jesus is referring to the desolation of the temple brought on by the Roman legions in 70 A.D. (Luke 21:20-24). However he ends those verses by speaking of the 'times of the Gentiles' needing to be fulfilled. This seems to be a clear reference to the church age when Israel is largely hardened even as God continues to work out his purposes through the overwhelmingly Gentile church (Romans 11:25). However in the ensuing verses of Luke 21, the Lord Jesus begins to speak in great detail of signs leading up to his glorious return. Thus it becomes quite evident that two events, albeit related, are in view.

Seeing the Olivet Discourse as a dual reference prophecy helps us understand why some parts of this discourse seem to refer to events that transpired only 40 years later and how other parts still await a future fulfillment. Remember Jesus had been posed with two questions by his disciples, one related to the destruction of the temple and one to his second coming. Thus he is essentially prophesying the imminent destruction of the temple in the life-time of those listening to him as a sign and ultimately a guarantee that his words regarding the second coming would likewise be fulfilled. So, instead of seeing the fulfillment of Jesus' words only in the first century or in the future we can see them essentially fulfilled in both.

The Birth Pains

In Matthew 24 Jesus goes on to list a number of

road markers or warning signs that would show us when we are getting near to the final destination. These include, false prophets, wars and rumors of wars, natural disasters, persecution, apostasy, signs in the heavens and more. Today as I write there are plenty of rumors of wars in the Middle East. The daily news is dominated by reports of earthquakes and potential tsunamis in East Asia, large-scale fires in the Mediterranean area and flooding all over Europe. There are also horrific stories of persecution from North Africa and Central Asia. Not to mention the on-going global threat of the Corona virus. Are we there yet?

When presented with the Biblical signs of the end times, many skeptics are quick to point out that such events have always dominated human history. What's new? How will be able to distinguish between the typical disasters that regularly rack humankind and the cataclysms leading to the end of times? In order to understand the signs I think we need to take stock of the bold hint that Jesus mentioned when he spoke of 'birth pains.'

I know a few things about birth pains, as much as a man can know at least. I had the privilege of being present for the birth of each of my three children in Turkey. Although that is standard procedure for most men in the West, in the Middle East, that took a minor miracle. Most women here are wheeled into the birthing section of the hospitals while the husbands stay outside for hours waiting to hear some news from their hapless wives.

In preparation for our first child's birth I read books with my wife and tried to prepare as much as possible for the adventure ahead. We found a doctor that spoke decent English and let him know that I expected to be let into the birthing room. When the time arrived, that was easier said than done. After a heated debate with the head nurse at the private hospital in Izmir, she finally let me in. It was a good thing I was there, because our doctor suddenly forgot all his English and started yelling 'pull' instead of 'push.'

For our second daughter's birth we were in rural Turkey. During one of our checkups I mentioned my desire to be at my wife's side during the birth to the head nurse; this she emphatically rejected. To make her point she let me peek into the labor lounge only to see a dozen or so women huffing and puffing in pain as they waddled around preparing for birth. Seeing a man in there would surely send them all to the birthing table, so my petition was out of the question. However, God was merciful and the day my wife's turn came the labor lounge was completely empty. Still the midwife insisted I not be allowed in. 'What do you know about birthing?' she demanded. I retorted that I had been keeping track of my wife's contractions, the length of each one and the intervals in between and that she was now a few centimeters dilated… She was duly impressed and let me in.

Now for those who don't know what I'm talking about, here is a short lesson in birth pains. Days before giving birth a pregnant woman will begin feeling short jabs of pain which young couples often misinterpret to mean that the birth is at hand. No! It is just the beginning and it gets much worse! As time goes on these 'pangs' will become more and more intense. At first they might happen infrequently but as the time approaches they become quite regular even as the time interval between them shortens. In short, leading up to the birth the mother feels more intense birth pangs even as they come more frequently.

In the middle of his discussion on the final signs Jesus said *'all these are but the beginning of the birth pains'* (24:8). The first point is obvious, we should not rush to conclusions too quickly. Secondly the 'signs' will need to grow in intensity even as the intervals between them shortens. In other words, even though there have always been earthquakes and famines, as we approach the end these will intensify and become more frequent. Indeed we are experiencing just such a 'speeding up' as natural catastrophes and political upheavals sweep the globe almost non-stop.

When we revisit the signs Jesus listed we can see the pattern clearly: The last century saw a massive proliferation of cults and false teachers coupled with gross moral failures in the church leading many to abandon the faith. The casualties from the world wars of the last century alone eclipse all previous chapters of human history. Despite being more wealthy and technologically advanced than ever before, today millions still go hungry and struggle to survive. Great strides have been made in political science as democracy has spread across the globe and yet thousands still flee from repressive regimes in the Middle East in order to seek haven in the West. Can it get any worse?

Actually the mention of birth pains reminds us of where everything began to go wrong. On account of human rebellion in the Garden of Eden God punished mankind and cursed the earth. Because of this, even as women were doomed to experience pain in childbirth, Paul reminds us that the whole creation continues to experience birth pangs. In other words the natural disasters that repeatedly rack our world are reminders of that curse. However they also serve to remind us that sooner or later these pains will reach their goal, namely *"the revealing of the sons of God"* (Romans 8:19-23). So we should not be surprised to see all of creation in upheaval as it prepares to give birth to Christ's kingdom.

Maybe the most troubling of the signs laid out by Jesus for the end times, are those that relate to believers. The church has always suffered persecution and it has ultimately served to strengthen her. However in the last days persecution takes on a whole new dimension as it is both global in scope and deeply personal in nature. In the Middle East I have often had to look on helplessly as a family tears into a young believer on account of their newfound faith in Christ. Words fail me in times like that. Then on the other side of the spectrum are western believers awash in their 'liberties' who know little of suffering for their faith. Christ warns that as lawlessness increases believer's love will decrease. What a striking contrast!

The final time leading up to the return of Christ will clearly be horrendous on a historic scale. However, even as the world spirals into complete chaos and wars rack the planet, God will continue to show mercy and save many. In fact

Jesus says that at this time the gospel of the kingdom will be proclaimed throughout the whole world as a testimony to all nations. Finally the great commission will be accomplished... then the end will come. We can see here a silver lining in the midst of the bleak darkness that characterizes the last days. Even as everything comes crashing down, untold millions will be turning to faith in Christ. So it will truly be like giving birth, the exhilaration of seeing Christ and his kingdom coming to fruition will somehow completely eclipse all the pain leading up to that moment.

The Seventy Sevens

Back in Matthew 24, after giving a list of the signs Jesus makes an allusion to something the Jewish people were evidently familiar with, namely the 'abomination of desolation.' He references the book of Daniel and urges the reader to go look it up in order to get the full picture. This is evidently something or someone innately sacrilegious who will take a stand in the temple. Jesus instructs believers when they see this happen, to flee for their lives. In fact he urges them run out of town like Lot leaving Sodom without looking back, because this abomination will usher in the great tribulation (24:21).

There are three references to this 'abomination' in the book of Daniel. The first sets the stage as it is placed in the final phase of God's program for Israel's redemption (Daniel 9:27). In the second reference the 'abomination' refers to a pagan idol of Zeus set up by the infamous Seleucid king Antiochus Epiphanes in the temple. At that time Antiochus banned Jewish sacrifices and instead offered a pig on God's altar in Jerusalem. This sparked the Maccabean revolt in the second century B.C (Daniel 11:31-32). This 'abomination' or desecration of the temple seems to prefigure and foreshadow the final abomination at the end of Israel's history described in the final chapter of Daniel as happening in the middle of a seven year tribulation (12:11).

To understand the detailed time frames revealed to Daniel at the end of his book, we need to first understand the prophetic calendar revealed in chapter 9. At the beginning of the chapter Daniel recognized that the 70 year exile predicted by Jeremiah was soon to be completed but he also realized that his people had not yet fully repented. Thus he takes it upon himself repent for them and to beseech God's mercy on their behalf. In response to his prayer the angel Gabriel arrives promising to give him insight into a vision of Israel's future. This vision encapsulates God's program for Israel's future.

> *"Seventy weeks are decreed about your people and your holy city, to finish the transgression, to put an end to sin, and to atone for iniquity, to bring in everlasting righteousness, to seal both vision and prophet, and to anoint a most holy place. Know therefore and understand that from the going out of the word to restore and build Jerusalem to the coming of an anointed one, a prince, there shall be seven weeks. Then for sixty-two weeks it shall be built again with squares and moat, but in a troubled time. And after the sixty-two weeks, an anointed one shall be cut off and shall have nothing. And the people of the prince who is to come shall destroy the city and the sanctuary. Its end shall come with a flood, and to the end there shall be war. Desolations are decreed. And he shall make a strong covenant with many for one week, and for half of the week he shall put an end to sacrifice and offering. And on the wing of abominations shall come one who makes desolate, until the decreed end is poured out on the desolator"* (Daniel 9:24-27).

The incredible detail outlined in this passage is truly stunning, making it one of the most remarkable prophecies of all time. Most scholars are agreed that by 70 weeks (heptads/sevens) Gabriel is speaking of a total of 490 years. Walvoord and Zuck note, "Whereas people today think in units of tens (decades), Daniel's people thought in terms of sevens (heptads). Seven days are in one week. Every seventh year was a sabbath rest year (Lev. 25:1-7). Seven 'sevens' brought them to the Year of Jubilee (Lev. 25:8-12). Seventy 'sevens,' then, is a span of 490 years."[14]

The stated purposes of this prophetic calendar in verse 24 clearly point to the yet future culmination of God's plans with regard to Israel in general and the temple in particular. Earlier in the chapter Daniel had been praying for the spiritual restoration of his people as well as the return to the land and the rebuilding of the temple, so God here explains in detail how his prayers will ultimately be answered. As most complex things in life it will not materialize all at once but rather will take place in several phases.

Gabriel goes on to divide Israel's prophetic calendar into three main segments. The first segment of 49 years (7 weeks) has often been overlooked and simply linked to the next section of 62 weeks[15] but it begs the question as to why it is listed separately in the prophecy. Likewise just as there is a substantial gap between the 62 weeks and the last week, we should expect a gap between the 7 weeks and the 62 weeks. Thus we are looking for a period of 49 years prior to the rebuilding of Jerusalem in the time of Nehemiah (440 B.C.).

The angel Gabriel makes it clear that the starting point for the first segment is *"the going out of the word to restore and build Jerusalem,"* and the end point is *"the coming of an anointed one, a prince."* What do these refer to? The mention of an 'anointed one' is intriguing, and although many might rush to link it the second mention of an 'anointed one' Jesus Christ in verse 26, it is clear that the latter one is placed after the 62 weeks. Who then is the first 'anointed one'? Earlier we saw how God promised to raise up a great leader named Cyrus to deliver the nation of Israel from exile. The prophet Isaiah specifically described him as being anointed for this specific task (Isaiah 45:1). He emerged on the world scene in 539 B.C. when he conquered Babylon. This is the same year that Daniel is recording this prophecy. In other words Gabriel is noting that the deliverance of the Jewish people from exile is indeed at hand.

God will answer Daniel's prayer right away, but how?

Indeed, soon after repenting on behalf of his people and receiving this vision, Daniel was confronted with a life-threatening decision. Darius, the new ruler of Babylon and likely the father in law of Cyrus, ill advisedly decreed that no one was allowed to pray to anyone but the king. Daniel, although having been hand picked for high office, refused to compromise his faith and instead chose to pay the ultimate price by going to the lion's den (Daniel 6). However it was on account of his faithfulness and subsequent miraculous deliverance from certain death that the eyes of the king were opened. In all likelihood this served as a catalyst to spur the Medo-Persian emperor Cyrus to declare the now famous edict allowing the Jewish people to return to their homeland and rebuild their temple (Ezra 1). In short, God used Daniel's great trial to answer his own prayer for Israel's deliverance and fulfill the divine decree written by Jeremiah. Watch out what you pray for...the answer might involve you!

So if the end point of the first 7 weeks is 539 B.C., then the beginning point would have been 49 years earlier at around 588 B.C. What was happening then? Those were the last couple of tragic years when Jerusalem was besieged by the Babylonian army pending its final destruction at the hands of Nebuchadnezzar in 586 B.C. At that time the prophet Jeremiah continued to warn his people of the coming judgment of God. However he also began to receive divine revelation pointing to the New Covenant age. Even as Babylon's noose tightened around Jerusalem and their tragic end loomed ever larger, Jeremiah predicted the future return of the exiles and the restoration of Israel (Jeremiah 33). Thus it was that 49 years prior to the coming of Cyrus, God had indeed decreed the rebuilding of Jerusalem even as it was about to be destroyed.

Understanding the first seven weeks of Daniel's prophecy in this manner may seem surprising to many who are used to viewing it sometime after the destruction of Babylon.[16] However, when the details of the prophecy are all considered, this interpretation seems to fit the historical context the best. It also makes better sense of why Gabriel told Daniel that his prayers had already been answered (Daniel 9:23). Indeed God had not forgotten his promise of deliverance given before the exile. Likewise we see how Jeremiah's faithfulness in that dark time of Israel's history was later beautifully complemented by Daniel's faithfulness while exiled in Babylon.

The Prince To Come

Now we come to the next two sections of Daniel's seventy week's prophecy in which he speaks of the 'abomination' referenced by Jesus in the Mount of Olives. In this regard it is important to note that the first and second section of this amazing prophecy would have been fulfilled quite literally by the time Jesus spoke of the impending destruction of Jerusalem to his disciples. Indeed, the fact that Old Testament prophecies like these have always been fulfilled with remarkable precision gives us every reason to believe that the portions that still await fulfillment will likewise fall into place with amazing exactitude.

The second and longest segment of the seventy weeks prophecy relates to the 434 years (62 weeks) which starts with the rebuilding of the city of Jerusalem. Daniel's text reads, *"it shall be built again with squares and moat, but in a troubled time."* This took place under the leadership of Nehemiah who was made governor of Jerusalem in the 20th year of the Persian king Artaxerxes (445-444 B.C). Although we often assume that Nehemiah went straight away to Jerusalem, Josephus notes that the rebuilding of Israel's capital city took place in the 25th year of the Persian king.[17] It is likely that it took some time for Nehemiah to put his affairs in order and make the long trip to Jerusalem or that he made an intervening trip. Once started, however, the actual reconstruction was finished in a record time of 52 days, even as they were harassed by their envious neighbors, just as Daniel foretold. Thus we can put the starting point of the second segment at 440 B.C.

Looking back to the text of the seventy weeks prophecy we notice that no terminus is provided for the second segment of 434 years. Daniel is simply told that after the 62 weeks are concluded the 'anointed one' would be cut off and have nothing. This is a clear reference to Jesus the Messiah. Thus it is not surprising that counting 434 years from 440 B.C. lands on 6 B.C. which corresponds precisely with the estimated date of the birth of Christ.[18] With regard to the 'anointed one', Daniel is told that he would be cut off, and left completely alone. This is a clear reference to the trial and crucifixion of Jesus in which he was abandoned by his followers and shouldered the world's sins all alone (Isaiah 53:5; Mark 9:12). This is a clear prediction of how Christ's first coming would end in his rejection and the postponement of God's plans.

Subsequent to this Daniel receives the sad news that the temple would once again be destroyed. This catastrophe is presumably connected to the rejection of the Messiah. Daniel is told that the whole city of Jerusalem and the sanctuary would be destroyed by the people of some future prince. Gabriel goes further saying that Jerusalem's end would come like a flood full of war leading to utter desolation. This correlates exactly with the prophecy of Christ in Matthew 24 about the destruction of the temple, all which took place in the years of the Jewish revolt (66-70 A.D.). But there is more, there is one week left in God's plans for Israel.[19]

SEVENTY WEEKS PROPHECY

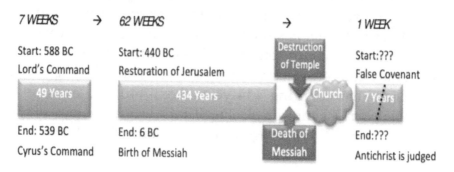

7 WEEKS → 62 WEEKS → 1 WEEK

Start: 588 BC
Lord's Command

49 Years

End: 539 BC
Cyrus's Command

Start: 440 BC
Restoration of Jerusalem

434 Years

End: 6 BC
Birth of Messiah

Destruction of Temple

Church

Death of Messiah

Start:???
False Covenant

7 Years

End:???
Antichrist is judged

In the final verse we are finally introduced to the aforementioned 'prince to come' and the 'abomination' he instigates. It has become commonplace for many commentators to assume he is Roman in origin as it was the Roman legions under the Roman General Titus that destroyed Jerusalem in 70 A.D. However it is critical to take careful note of Daniel's first reference to him in 9:26. He expressly says that the *people* of the yet future prince are responsible for the destruction of the temple in 70 A.D. A careful analysis of the legions used to assail Jerusalem shows that they were not European in origin but rather largely Middle Eastern from the province of Roman Syria. Likewise, first century historians Tacitus and Josephus both stress that a sizable contingent of Arabs joined in the fray because of their great hatred of the Jews.[20] This means that we should not necessarily look for the 'prince to come' to emerge in Europe but rather in the Middle East.

Daniel 9:27 describes this end times' 'prince' as the ultimate enemy of Israel who will make a seven year covenant with 'the many' or the lords (Hb: Rabim). Many assume this refers exclusively to Israel but quite to the contrary, the text seems to indicate a broader treaty or pact among neighboring nations. In all likelihood this covenant includes Israel because the subject of agreement is a rebuilt temple presumably in Jerusalem. However, in the middle of this period, after three and a half years, the 'prince who is to come' suddenly puts an end to sacrifices at the temple and does something abominable.

What exactly this end time leader does at the temple is subject to much speculation. The word 'abomination' here is elsewhere used to describe something idolatrous, detestable and/or filthy (1 Kings 11:5, 7; 2 Kings 23:13). Daniel is only told that this abomination takes place on the 'wing' or 'pinnacle' of the temple and that it involves that 'one' who makes desolate[21] the temple, presumably the 'prince', the chief instigator of this desecration. The closest historical parallel to this is found in the aforementioned temple desecration instigated by Antiochus Epiphanes in the 167 B.C. The apostle Paul sheds some more light on this in his description of the antichrist in 2 Thessalonians 2, but more on this later. Although the details of the abomination in Daniel are unclear what is eminently clear is that the utter destruction of this final challenger of God has been decreed. In the end he and his reign will be utterly demolished and God's kingdom will prevail.

The Tribulation

The 70 Week prophecy establishes some important parameters that help set up our eschatological framework. It clearly speaks to a yet future seven year segment initiated by the making of some geopolitical treaty related to Israel and the temple. This time frame is further confirmed by many Biblical passages speaking to the final three and a half years or 42 months of a time of great distress culminating with the coming of Jesus Christ (Daniel 7:25, 12:7, 11; Revelation 11:2-3, 12:6, 14, 13:5). In Matthew 24, it is the 'abomination' that takes place at the temple in the mid-point of this final seven year segment to which Jesus directed his disciples. He went on to describe the subsequent period as the 'great tribulation', a time of unprecedented calamity (Matthew 24:21).

Jesus goes on to reiterate his warnings against false

prophets and counterfeit Messiahs. He warns his disciples against believing news regarding some covert appearance or mystical return of Christ. He also urges them not to be swayed by signs and wonders expressly designed to mislead the elect of God. Finally he reminds them that his second appearing will not be an undercover operation, rather the sign of the Son of Man will appear in the heavens like lightning for all the world to see and recognize.

Before elaborating on his second coming, Jesus leaves his disciples with one more cryptic sign: *'Wherever the corpse is, there the vultures will gather.'* Jesus here gives a specific location as to where these events will transpire (Luke 17:37). Jewish people familiar with Old Testament prophetic writings would have likely connected this to the vivid description of carnage and carrion in Ezekiel 39:17-21. That famous passage on Gog and Magog correlates closely with the New Testament description of the battle of armageddon (Revelation 19:17-18). Most importantly these passages all point to Israel and more specifically to Jerusalem as the great stage upon which the final battle will play out (Zechariah 14).

In these verses Jesus is clearly not just speaking of the historic destruction of the temple in 70 A.D. but also to some greater fulfillment in the future culminating in his bodily return to earth. When we understand this discourse as dual fulfillment we can see how Jesus was using the imminent destruction of the temple as a template for the greater desecration to come in the end. Indeed, just as Antiochus Epiphanes' earlier abominable desecration of the temple in 167 B.C., the Roman legions in 70 A.D., led by General Titus, also sacked Jerusalem and finally demolished the temple.

Regarding the fall of the second temple, it is important to note that the fourth century church historian Eusebius specifically links this tragic event to the prophetic words of Jesus regarding the destruction of the temple. He further quotes extensively from the Jewish historian Josephus, detailing the horrific scenes that unfolded during this time, attributing them ultimately to God's judgment declared by Jesus 40 years previously. He describes how many of the signs laid out in the Olivet discourse indeed happened, such that the Jerusalem church took heed of Jesus' warnings and fled to Pella thus avoiding the impending destruction.[22]

However, it must be noted that while Eusebius and earlier church fathers saw in the destruction of the temple a fulfillment of Christ's prophecies, they also believed that his second coming, preceded by a time of tribulation and culminating in his millennial reign, was still in the cards. They clearly recognized that while the events of 70 A.D. partially aligned with Christ's predictions, they did not represent the fullness of his prophecies because they did not result in the physical return of Christ. Consequently the destruction of the second temple serves as a precursor and pattern for the yet future conflagration in the last days.

Likewise, when we look at the seminal texts on the 'abomination' referenced by Jesus in the book of Daniel, we can see the different phases of fulfillment as they play out in history. First the temple was desecrated by Antiochus Epiphanes in 167 B.C. Later the temple was actually demolished by Titus in 70 A.D. Both of these events constituted an abomination leading to desolation. They further set the mold for the final 'abomination' predicted by Christ to take place in the middle of the yet future great tribulation which would be characterized by desecration and then final destruction.

These and other passages make it clear that yet another temple will need to be built in Jerusalem before the return of Christ. It is in this future temple that the antichrist will take his seat and declare himself to be a deity (2 Thessalonians 2:4). As I write these words there is no Jewish temple in Jerusalem, although preparations to build one have been underway for many years. The problem is that the historic site of the temple is currently occupied by an Islamic shrine, the Dome of the Rock. How or when a new temple will be built is a looming question, but we can be confident based on God's Word that before the end, this sign will also materialize.

Furthermore, based on Christ's predictions, we are to expect this future temple once built, to likewise be desecrated at the mid-point of the tribulation period and ultimately destroyed. As in the previous conflagration of 70 A.D., as reported by Josephus, we can expect these events to be accompanied by natural disasters, signs in the heavens, false prophets, massacres and military confrontations. In this final fulfillment, we can further expect all the signs described by Jesus in Matthew 24 will indeed take place quite literally.

To summarize, we can see that Christ's predictions of the destruction of the temple had a two-fold fulfillment. While the preliminary fulfillment in 70 A.D. served as an example and guarantee of the yet future fulfillment, it is clear that this latter one will ultimately take place in the context of the final seven year tribulation prophesied by Daniel. At that time, the scope and scale of the catastrophic events related to God's judgment of the earth will make all previous cataclysms pale in comparison. The details of these divine judgments are further spelled out in Revelation 6-18 and will be discussed later.

The Parousia

After discussing the signs indicative of the great tribulation Jesus keys into the main event, namely his appearing or arrival (Gk. Parousia). He emphasizes that this will take place 'immediately after the tribulation.' At that time all of creation will revolt as it did at Christ's crucifixion, signaling the end. Descriptions of the cataclysmic events surrounding the Lord's return abound in the Old Testament (Isaiah 24:23; Joel 2:10, 31, 3:15; Zephaniah 1:15). These appear in the context of the great 'Day of the Lord' in which God finally intervenes to deliver his people and establish his kingdom. They are further echoed in many New Testament passages, especially in the judgments described in the book of Revelation (2 Peter 3:10; Revelation

6:12-17, 16:10).

At that time the 'sign of the Son of Man' will appear in the heavens resulting in great mourning. The mourning is likely a reference to Israel's mourning and repentance described earlier. In the introduction of the Revelation John describes the main event of the book as follows: *'Behold, he is coming with the clouds, and every eye will see him, even those who pierced him, and all tribes of the earth will wail on account of him. Even so. Amen'* (Revelation 1:7). Even as he speaks of all tribes and nations suffering deep anxiety as they see Christ in the clouds readying for his return to earth, he highlights the abject grief of 'those who pierced him,' namely the Jewish people.

The 'sign of the Son of Man' mentioned here is intriguing. This reference immediately takes us back to Daniel's vision:

> *I saw in the night visions, and behold, with the clouds of heaven there came one like a son of man, and he came to the Ancient of Days and was presented before him. And to him was given dominion and glory and a kingdom, that all peoples, nations, and languages should serve him; his dominion is an everlasting dominion, which shall not pass away, and his kingdom one that shall not be destroyed* (Daniel 7:13-14).

Daniel chapter 7 gives a detailed description of consecutive kingdoms which impact Israel and are centered in the Middle East. After the final beast is destroyed, the kingdom of earth is entrusted to the Son of Man. Jesus often appropriated this title and even quoted this passage in his final defense before the Sanhedrin (Matthew 26:64). There he noted that his accusers would see the Son of Man *'seated at the right hand of Power and coming on the clouds of heaven.'* In short he was stating that one day the roles would be reversed and they would be in the hot seat being judged by him.

Likewise, his words also give us a hint as to the 'sign of the Son of Man.' Jesus seems to be intimating that his enemies will indeed see him seated at the right hand of God's throne receiving the kingdom. This will evidently take place in the clouds previous to his final decent to earth. Although Christ is already seated at the right hand of his Father in heaven, as described in Psalm 110, the rest of the psalm speaks of him being further enthroned in Zion as King and eternal Priest, even as he prepares to descend to earth and vanquish his enemies. Interestingly this all takes place as his people *"offer themselves freely on the day of his power"* (Psalm 110:3). Thus it seems that when the Jewish nation in particular finally recognizes Jesus as their Messiah, he will initiate his final decent to earth in order to take his place on David's throne and be crowned King of Kings.

Luke's account of this climactic moment in history highlights the intense fear and foreboding that will sweep over Christ's enemies at the sudden appearance of him in the clouds:

> *And there will be signs in sun and moon and stars, and on the earth distress of nations in perplexity because of the roaring of the sea and the waves, people fainting with fear and with foreboding of what is coming on the world. For the powers of the heavens will be shaken. And then they will see the Son of Man coming in a cloud with power and great glory. Now when these things begin to take place, straighten up and raise your heads, because your redemption is drawing near* (Luke 21:25-28).

Matthew indicates that at this time the angels will be sent out to to gather God's elect from the four corners of the earth. This will be announced by a loud trumpet blast; more on this later as to how it might relate to the rapture. Thus at Christ's appearing in the clouds he will gather all believers to himself in preparation for his final descent to earth. Scriptures also point to this being the time when the great marriage supper of the lamb will take place (Revelation 19:7-9). Likewise, all believers, including those from the Old/First Covenant period, will be resurrected in order to take their place at the great heavenly banquet (Matthew 8:11). It is also likely that the famed 'judgment seat of Christ' in which he purifies and adorns his bride will also take place during this interim (Romans 14:10-12; 2 Corinthians 5:10). The Bible seems to imply that all these extraordinary events will be visible from earth which will cause the Jewish people to mourn on one hand and the Lord's enemies to chafe on the other (Revelation 1:7).

At this time, even as the Lord Jesus finally seals the New Covenant with his bride in the clouds of heaven and with all the world as his witness, the true heavenly nature of the church will finally be visible to all (1 John 3:1-2). Creation will also rejoice at the 'revealing of the sons of God,' in expectation of the immanent return of Christ and restoration of the planet (Romans 8:19). At this time the Jewish people in particular, will finally mourn for the one they have pierced and wholeheartedly welcome his imminent return (Zechariah 12:10). Thus, Christ will commence his triumphal return to the earth, specifically with a view to deliver the embattled nation of Israel.

Joel Richardson, in his exhaustive treatment of this subject in his book *Sinai to Zion*, makes a convincing argument from the desert prophecies pointing to Christ's return starting from Mt. Sinai as he retraces the route of the Exodus. In doing so he regathers his exiled people and makes his way to Bozrah (East of Israel in modern Jordan), where he single-handedly vanquishes their enemies (Isaiah 63:1-6). Finally his feet will rest on the Mount of Olives, the same place Jesus was giving this discourse and was later taken into heaven (Acts 1). The prophet Zechariah paints the final picture as follows:

> *Then the LORD my God will come, and all the holy ones with him. On that day there shall be no light, cold, or frost. And there shall be a unique day, which is known to the LORD, neither day nor night, but at evening time there shall be light. On that day living waters shall flow out from Jerusalem, half of them to the eastern sea and half of them to the western sea. It shall continue in summer as in winter. And the LORD will be king over all the earth. On that day the LORD will be one and his name one... And this shall be the plague with which the LORD*

will strike all the peoples that wage war against Jerusalem: their flesh will rot while they are still standing on their feet, their eyes will rot in their sockets, and their tongues will rot in their mouths. And on that day a great panic from the LORD shall fall on them, so that each will seize the hand of another, and the hand of the one will be raised against the hand of the other (Zechariah 14:5b-9, 12-13).

The final and overwhelming victory of Christ over his enemies is further described in Revelation 19. In that passage Christ is pictured as the righteous judge and King of all Kings, riding a white stallion as he returns to earth followed by his entourage. More on this in the last chapter. In short, the final arrival or parousia of the Lord Jesus is amply attested throughout Scripture and presented as the apex of God's purposes on earth.

Conclusion

All the signs ultimately point to Jesus. The tragic history of mankind will finally be reversed in the kingdom of Christ. Like the early believers who eagerly awaited his glorious appearing, we should likewise be attentive to the signs showing the way to the end, as laid out by the Lord Jesus himself. Although we may not yet be able to ascertain with complete certainty some of the details relating to the last days, God's Word provides us with a roadmap that will guide us as we enter those troubled times. Then as we move forward in faith we should be able to recognize more readily the signs previously spelled out by Jesus.

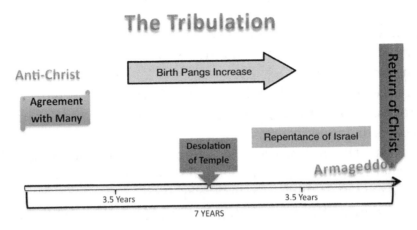

Here is a summary of the signs we have discussed based on Christ's prophecy given on the Mount of Olives and related passages:

- The antichrist will establish a seven year pact with Israel and its neighbors related to a rebuilt temple in Jerusalem. False prophets will proliferate.
- People's lifestyles in the end times will be reminiscent of the gross immorality of Noah and Lot's time. They will live carefree lives and curse God at every corner.
- Increased wickedness across the globe will result in decreased love for God and even apostasy, namely wholesale abandonment of the Christian faith.
- At the mid-point of the tribulation the temple in Jerusalem will be desecrated by the 'abomination' and later destroyed even as the Jewish people are forced to flee for their lives.
- During this time some from the nation of Israel will repent for their rejection of the Messiah and the gospel of Jesus Christ will go out to the ends of the earth.
- In the ensuing global revival, believers worldwide will suffer unprecedented persecution by their own family members and hostile regimes.
- Despite earlier promises of peace and prosperity the world will

now descend into abject chaos as wars and rumors of wars proliferate.

- Natural disasters including earthquakes, famines and plagues will increase in number and intensity creating consternation the world over.
- Strange portents and terrifying signs in the heavens will cause great confusion, along with miracle workers inspired by Satan who will deceive many.
- Toward the end of the great tribulation, the antichrist will gather many armies to Israel and threaten to obliterate those who are left of God's people in Jerusalem.
- The sign of the Son of Man will suddenly be visible to all mankind as he appears in the clouds. Christ will be given the kingdom of earth even as he is seen enthroned at the right hand of God in the clouds.
- Simultaneously, the Lord Jesus will gather believers both dead and alive from all over the earth unto himself.
- As we reach the end, the heavenly bodies will be snuffed out even as all manner of cataclysmic events transpire when God pours out the fullness of his wrath on earth.
- The nation of Israel will finally recognize the one they have pierced and repent as one, thus opening the way for Christ's return to earth.
- Jesus Christ will descend from heaven with all the heavenly hosts and his resurrected people and make his way to Jerusalem to destroy his enemies and establish his long-awaited kingdom.

We noted that these signs are described by Jesus as 'birth pains.' This helps us differentiate between the 'normal' trials the world has always faced and the tribulation trials we should expect in the future. In the latter the 'pains' will be much like birth pangs where they increase in intensity even as they shorten in interval. Thus when wars, earthquakes and other cataclysmic events begin to proliferate we will know the end game is fast approaching.

When interpreting the signs laid out in the Olivet discourse many modern scholars are eager to see them as having been fulfilled already in the events surrounding the destruction of Jerusalem in 70 A.D. Others like to see them as being fulfilled only in the future time of the great tribulation. We noted however, that this text is best interpreted in light of the Biblical principle of dual fulfillment. In other words, Jesus was speaking in reference both to the destruction of the temple in the short term, and its yet future desecration leading up to the parousia. Again a 'both/and' interpretation seems to fit the context best.

The preliminary fulfillment of Jesus' prophecy took place in the life-time of those hearing him when they witnessed the destruction of the temple in 70 A.D. The ultimate fulfillment of his prophecy however, awaits the rebuilding of the temple and its subsequent desecration in the mid-point of the seven year tribulation period, paving the way for the return of Christ. The partial fulfillment of Jesus' words within the life-span of those hearing him served as a guarantee of its ultimate fulfillment in the second coming. Thus, two thousand years later, having seen how Christ's words were initially fulfilled in the complete demolition of the temple under the Romans, we can have complete confidence that the remainder his promises regarding his second coming will soon find their ultimate fulfillment.

5. THE BEAST

After being kicked out of Turkey in 2013, partly for writing 'The Beast Awakens' article mentioned earlier, our family settled in North Cyprus. We soon realized that the northern one-third of the island, known as the Turkish Republic of North Cyprus, largely sustains itself by attracting students from around the Middle East to study in English and ultimately propel themselves to the West. After helping in an English teaching effort at the local university our first summer on the island, I was offered a full scholarship to study at the Eastern Mediterranean University.

It was a hard offer to reject, but it was harder to find a subject I would be interested in studying. I finally decided on pursuing a Master's in International Relations with a focus on political science of the Middle East. Soon I found myself in a classroom with a group of head-strong activists from around the region. Hearing first-hand their perspective on how western intervention in the Middle East has negatively affected their lives and societies, was enlightening to say the least. Although most of our textbooks, written by western scholars, touted the global benefits of democracy, it was clear from my life experience in this region and that of the Middle Eastern students around me that the democratic experiment had failed miserably, particularly in this part of world.

When it came time to write my thesis I chose to tackle the subject of democracy in the Middle East head-on. However, instead of parroting western opinions or floating my own I wanted to give voice to the students around me, many of whom had personally endured the 'Arab Spring' and seen the effects of the 'War on Terror' in their home countries. I prepared a questionnaire regarding the subject and interviewed a representative sample of sixteen Middle Easterners. Their answers painted a stark picture, proving again to me that there was indeed a great disconnect between Middle Eastern perception of democracy and the idilic version the West was trying to export to them. Moreover it pointed to Islam as the chief culprit for the ongoing upheavals in their countries, because the tenets of the Quran are ultimately incompatible with liberal democracy and secular governance espoused by the West.

When the time came to defend my thesis to the university board of professors, one of whom was an American and the other two nominal Muslim Turks, they did not take kindly to my conclusions. Entrenched as they were in liberal scholasticism, they did not want to acquiesce to the failure of western democracy or the critical role Islam plays in deterring good governance in the Middle East. In the end however, they could not dispute my methodology and the fact that my thesis presented empirical evidence based on the shared experiences of Middle Easterners. Those interested in the final form of my thesis can find it on Amazon under the title, *Democracy in the Middle East: An Indigenous Assessment.*

After my three years of 'higher' education in a secular institution, I became more convinced than ever of the moral and political bankruptcy of western ideals touted by foreign governments trying to 'save' the world by exporting democracy to the ends of the planet. It also served to confirm for me once more the central role Islam plays in countering the prospect of true freedom and global peace. More than anything, my brief reconnaissance of the secular landscape and liberal worldview underscored to me the Biblical truth that only Jesus can set things right in the world. All the democratic theorizing of secular scholars and political pundits has only led the world to a dark dead end. Indeed, the kingdom of our Lord is the only hope for the world.

Even as we wait eagerly for the Lord's return and watch all the efforts of the almighty West come to naught, we are reminded of all the Biblical injunctions relating to the final human kingdom. From the dawn of history humankind has tried over and over to establish governments that ensure their people's peace and prosperity. Like the first kingdom of Babylon, all of these have ultimately found themselves in direct opposition to God's rule and reign, being as they are, under the tutelage of Satanic powers. The Bible makes it clear that as we enter the final stage of human history, one last desperate attempt will be made by Satan to establish world dominion. But this last kingdom and its leader, the antichrist, is also doomed to failure.

Ever since the prophets predicted the rise and fall of the last kingdom, characterized as 'The Beast', many have tried to ascertain its identity, but most have proven short-sighted. Why is this? Firstly, because, like the signs we noted earlier, while we are able gather many clues as to his character and kingdom from the Scriptures, positive identification of the antichrist will only be possible when he arrives on the scene. Secondly, it must be noted that all Bible interpreters, in our attempts to connect the prophetic dots, unwittingly read into the Scriptures our own biases and naturally seek to find a correlation in the political landscape of our day. For example many western believers living in the time of World War II were quick to associate the Beast with Adolf Hitler. During the Cold War it was easy to read Russia into our end times' scenarios. Historically others have attempted to connect the beast to the Catholic Church or more recently to the European Union. The reality is that most of these speculations have effectively become smoke screens obstructing our vision from where the true danger lies.

In this regard it is important to get re-centered in our vision of the future. As noted before, one of the critical rules of prophecy that we must always keep in mind as we seek to match the text with current events, is the fact that the Bible presents prophecy from a Jewish perspective and as it relates specifically to her future. Thus in our analysis of today's events we must look specifically for those matters that relate to Israel and its neighbors.

The Beast From The Sea

The Bible is full of details related to the identity of the final human kingdom and its ruler, the antichrist. However these are scattered throughout the Scriptures and need to be pieced together carefully. In many ways it's like studying a crime scene frozen in time, only it has yet to happen. Finding the clues is not enough, knowing what to look for and establishing the connection between them is essential to solving the riddle. In this regard it is often easiest to start with the most obvious evidence available and work our way backward. In the book of Revelation we find much of the evidence already put together for us as it pulls together material from all over the Bible.

In Revelation 13 the apostle John is shown a beast that comes out of the sea, presumably the Mediterranean Sea, which has ten horns and seven heads. We first note that this beast is almost a mirror image of the dragon described earlier in Revelation 12:3, which clearly represents the 'old serpent' Satan, the only difference being the number of crowns they wear. Still, it is clear that the beast is tailored after the dragon and is empowered by him. From the description provided the beast seems to be a composite of all the beasts/kingdoms described in Daniel chapter 7. One of the most striking features of this beast is that one of its heads has received a fatal blow which later is healed and becomes the source of great amazement in the world. The significance of this comes to light later in Revelation 17.

This beast is further described as one who wages war in such a way that he is unrivaled and thus earns the admiration and adulation of the nations. The beast is also characterized by a 'boastful mouth' just as is the little horn in Daniel 7. Likewise it receives authority to rule for 42 months, namely 3 and a half years, a time also specified in Daniel 7:25 and 12:7 as relating to the final half of the great tribulation. John goes on to note that the beast specifically blasphemes God and his tabernacle and particularly wars against the saints. In this effort he is joined by peoples of every tribe and nation. Ultimately he becomes the object of worship for many people even as the God's people are said to suffer greatly at his hand.

A brief note must be made here with regard to John's assertion that 'all who dwell on earth will worship' the antichrist (Revelation 13:8). This has led many to think that this final world leader will somehow establish a global government in which all nations are somehow brought under his authority. This has further been popularized by many end times' books and movies. However, a careful assessment of the relevant Biblical texts reminds us that the antichrist will have many who will oppose him, including Egypt and Israel (Daniel 11). Furthermore, the fact that his kingdom is founded on 10 nations signifies a limit to his authority and implies he is not the 'King of the World.' Thus it seems best to interpret John's statement as hyperbolic, implying that people the world over will admire and likely live in tremendous fear of the antichrist.

Most commentators are unanimous in their assessment that the beast that comes from the sea is a description of the antichrist and his final kingdom. It has also been common to interpret the beast described here as a 'revived Roman Empire.'[23] Because of this much effort has gone into finding a fitting candidate for the end times' antichrist in Europe or Rome more specifically. However a closer look at the text and its own interpretation in chapter 17 actually urge us to look beyond Rome.

The fact that the beast arises from the sea is likely an indicator that he represents the Gentile nations opposed to Israel, as the sea was often used by the prophets as a symbol of the pagan peoples around them (Revelation 17:15). In contrast to this the second beast is described as coming from 'the land', maybe a clue to his possible Jewish identity. The latter beast is specifically charged with the duty of promoting the cause of the first beast and does so by performing great signs and wonders on his behalf. He likewise sets up some kind of speaking statue which may correlate with the 'abomination of desolation' set up in the temple as discussed earlier. The second beast further enforces an economic system based on the number of the beast's name 666. He is subsequently described as a 'false prophet' as he works miracles and strives to deceive the nations (Revelation 19:20). More on this when we discuss the Revelation.

To further ascertain the identity of the first beast we must turn our attention to Revelation 17. There we come across the same beast only here it is described as scarlet in color[24] and carrying a harlot. The harlot is later described as a mystery named *"Babylon the Great"* which is, according to final verse of the chapter, first and foremost representative of a particular city and its pagan beliefs and immoral practices (Revelation 17:18). This great end time city is likely the capital of the antichrist's empire, however, it also fittingly represents the perpetuation of all world empires from the time of Babel to the end.

Exactly which city will fit this end times' role is yet to be seen. Babylon, the whore, is clearly also a metaphorical description, contrasting the antichrist's vile kingdom with the pure bride of Christ (Revelation 21). If we understand the antichrist's kingdom being rooted in the Middle East, it seems best to expect one of the great regional capitals like Baghdad or Istanbul to play this gruesome role in the last days. In fact, some have suggested that Babylon might literally be rebuilt for this very purpose while others make a convincing case for Mecca fitting the bill.[25] In the end, whatever city becomes home to the antichrist's empire, this mystery Babylon will meet its rightful end by being both devoured by its own patrons and destroyed by God (Revelation 14:8, 17:16-18).

The Revived Empire

Aside from depicting for us the great harlot, chapter 17 of Revelation gives us the most important clues about the identity of the antichrist.

The beast that you saw was, and is not, and is about to rise from the bottomless pit and go to destruction. And the dwellers on earth whose names have not been written in the book of life from the foundation of the world will marvel to see the beast, because it was and is not and is to come. This calls for a mind with wisdom: the seven heads are seven mountains on which the woman is seated; they are also seven kings, five of whom have fallen, one is, the other has not yet come, and when he does come he must remain only a little while. As for the beast that was and is not, it is an eighth but it belongs to the seven, and it goes to destruction. And the ten horns that you saw are ten kings who have not yet received royal power, but they are to receive authority as kings for one hour, together with the beast. These are of one mind, and they hand over their power and authority to the beast (Revelation 17:8-13).

Here the angel begins to decode the identity of the beast by stating three times that it *"was, and is not, and is about to come."* The text expressly states that the beast comes *"out of the abyss"* either a reference to the fact that it is empowered by Satan himself or to his possible resurrection from the dead, or potentially both. It further notes that he is headed to destruction. Finally it notes that unbelievers in particular will wonder at the fact that the beast who once was destroyed has somehow made an amazing comeback.

In the next verses the text states very clearly that the seven heads of the beast represent seven hills upon which the harlot, namely the city of the antichrist's kingdom, is established. Most ancient cities were built on prominent hills, including Rome and Istanbul, which were built on seven hills. The angel further states that the seven heads also represent seven kings and/or their kingdoms.[26] He says that five of these have fallen, one is, and one is yet to come. The *"one that is"* serves as our reference point as it clearly represents the Roman Empire which ruled in the time of the apostle John as he was receiving this vision. The five that have fallen must then represent those empires previous to Rome that ruled the Middle East and specifically had dealings with Israel, namely: Egypt, Assyria, Babylon, Medo/Persia and Greece. Of the 7th king that follows Rome, the angel says: *'The other has not yet come and when he comes he must remain a little while.'* The question then is, what is the 7th kingdom that comes after Rome?

Most people mistakenly believe that the Roman Empire ceased when the city of Rome was sacked and conquered by warring tribes in 476 A.D. However the fact is that the capital of the Roman Empire was transferred to Constantinople early in the fourth century and the Byzantine Empire based therein continued the Roman legacy for another 1000 years. This ended in 1453 A.D. when the Turkish hordes stormed Constantinople and established what came to be known as the Ottoman Empire. When we take stock of the empires of the Middle East described in Revelation 17, it seems best to see the Ottoman Empire, the late champion of Islam in the Middle East and the great menace of Europe for much of the past millennium, as the fulfillment of the predicted seventh empire that would come after Rome.

Many will be surprised by this conclusion as they are used to interpreting this seventh head as a 'revived Roman Empire.' However verse eleven goes on to give us one of the most critical clues towards identifying the antichrist's kingdom saying, *'As for the beast that was and is not, it is an eighth but it belongs to the seven.'* This verse stresses that it is the eighth king/kingdom which is revived, not the seventh. The text is further clear in referencing the beast or antichrist as an eighth king/kingdom but intimately related to the previous empire. This rules out the Roman Empire which was the sixth empire. If any empire is going to be revived and serve as a platform for the antichrist it would be the last one, the Islamic/Ottoman Empire.

The text further suggests that the seventh empire comes to a sudden end and yet is somehow revived. This seems to correlate with what was said in chapter 13 about the head that received a fatal wound and later being miraculously healed. Thus it speaks of the antichrist as being an eighth ruler and yet one and the same with the seventh kingdom. Thus we should expect to see the antichrist arise from the ruins of the Islamic/Ottoman Empire which came to a catastrophic end in World War I. The question now is this: Are there any signs of this last great Middle Eastern empire reviving?

In 1923, after the end of World War I, the Turkish general Mustafa Kemal Ataturk managed to salvage the modern Republic of Turkey from the ashes of the defunct Ottoman Empire. He sought to rebuild his nation's identity on a modern secular foundation rooted in Turkishness rather than Islam. On account of this he abolished the Caliphate (head of Islam) and introduced western education and dress code, among other innovations. Any resurgence of Islam was to be held in check by the military establishment, which did so, enacting several successful coups in the 20th century. But alas, early in the 21 century, an Islamic party managed to gain a foothold in Turkish politics and has since sought to recast the Republic of Turkey along a revived notion of Ottomanism. They have further made overtures to other Middle Eastern countries seeking to revive the Islamic Empire.

The remaining verses of Revelation 17 explain that the ten horns of the final beast represent ten kings that receive power together with the final ruler. These will lay the foundation for the final kingdom of the antichrist. Looking forward, any sign of ten kings or kingdoms forming a political coalition in the Middle East should alert us to a potential end time's beast on the horizon. However to get the fuller picture we now need to return to the passages alluded to in the Revelation.

Daniel's Dreadful Beast

The connection between the beast described in Revelation and the one described centuries earlier by the prophet Daniel is unmistakable. At the time, when Daniel was living in Babylon serving under several pagan kings, he was privy to many visions and dreams regarding the future of Israel and the nations. In chapter 7, Daniel sees a vision which portrays the human empires governing in the Middle East as a series of rapacious beasts. The forthcoming interpretation makes it evident that the lion represents the Babylonian Empire and the bear represents the subsequent Medo-Persian Empire. The identification of the third creature, the winged leopard, however, is a bit more complicated.

The final dreadful beast is clearly a precursor to the beast in Revelation 13 and seems to represent the kingdom which is home to the antichrist. According to our study of Revelation 17 this final beast seems to be a revived Islamic/Ottoman Empire which came after the Roman/Byzantine Empire and will pave the way for the antichrist. This raises the question of the identity of the third beast before it. Does it represent the empire before the Islamic/Ottoman Empire, namely Rome or the one following the second beast, namely Greece. I believe it encapsulates both in one.

The historical Greco-Roman connection is evident in their shared ethnic, cultural and political similarities. Much like the previous Medo-Persian Empire, the Greeks and Romans were closely affiliated so much so that when the Romans established their empire they did so on the cultural and legal foundation laid by the Greeks. In fact history shows that they never conquered the Greeks but rather assimilated them. Because of this, during the Roman Empire, the global language of trade remained Koine Greek, because this allowed Rome to benefit greatly from the western civilization widely propagated by their Hellenic precursors. Likewise, as noted earlier, once the Western Roman Empire fell into decay, the Greeks to the east once again took to the helm of the empire in what is known as the Byzantine or Eastern Roman Empire.[27] In short, from beginning to end the fates and fortunes of the Greek and Romans were intertwined.

What is of greatest interest to us and to Daniel however, is the final beast, the antichrist's kingdom, which is described as *"dreadful, terrifying and extremely strong"* (Daniel 7:7). Later in the verse it speaks of this beast as having 10 horns just like the beast in Revelation 13. Then another horn arises among these and uproots three of them evidently establishing itself as the ruler of them all. This one is notorious for its human eyes and boastful mouth. This last world leader also excels at waging war against the saints and creating terror the world over.

Later in the chapter Daniel seeks an explanation of this final beast and the little horn in particular. Starting in verse 23 we read that this fourth beast is a fourth kingdom that will rule the earth. As noted earlier the Islamic/Ottoman Empire vanquished the Greeks and Romans when they finally conquered Constantinople (modern Istanbul), the historic capital of Christianity, in 1453. As Daniel predicted the reign of the Sultans was indeed *"different from all the previous kingdoms"* not simply because they *"devoured and trampled the whole earth,"* regularly launching military campaigns into eastern Europe and Asia, but more so because they broke it into pieces. Unlike previous empires which were somewhat homogeneous, the Ottoman Empire was largely characterized by ethnic fragmentation. The ruling Ottoman Turks themselves were a collection of tribes who immigrated from east Asia and likewise ruled over a patchwork of 'millets' or ethnic people groups.[28]

Verse 24 deals with the 'little horn' separately as it relates to the next and final phase of this last empire's world dominion. This is characterized by ten horns/kings out of which the 'little horn' emerges triumphant. Most commentators are agreed in seeing this little horn as representing the antichrist. The little horn subdues three of the ten kings establishing his supremacy.

He is also notorious for speaking out against the true God and warring against His people. The saints are subjected to his reign for three and a half years. In the end the Son of Man appears and defeats the impostor and finally takes back the kingdom on behalf of God's people.

In these verses we can see a clear parallel to what the apostle John described in Revelation 17. The final beast seems to point to the kingdom after the Byzantine/Eastern Roman Empire, namely the Islamic/Ottoman Empire, which is seen as later reviving and preparing the way for the antichrist through a coalition of 10 rulers/princes.

What is further noteworthy is the close correlation between the vision of Daniel in chapter 7 and the previous dream of King Nebuchadnezzar in chapter 2. The Babylonian King had a dream of a megalithic statue composed of different materials. Later Daniel interpreted the dream as follows: The golden head represents the kingdom of Babylon he served in. The silver chest and arms represents the Medo-Persian Empire to come afterwards. Based on our understanding of Daniel 7 and Revelation 17, the bronze mid-section and thighs in turn likely represents the Greco-Roman Empire. The iron legs likewise represent the Islamic/Ottoman Empire adept at crushing and shattering those in its domain. Thus the fourth kingdom in both Daniel 2 and 7, ultimately point to the Islamic/Ottoman Empire which later lays the foundation for the final reign of the antichrist.

The feet of the great statue Daniel 2, described as a mixture of iron and clay, should especially catch our attention. Here there is clearly a continuation of the iron from the previous phase, namely we are speaking essentially of the same empire but with new elements mixed in. Furthermore, the ten toes correlate perfectly with the ten horns/kings of Daniel 7 and Revelation 17. The next verses describe the feet and toes as being a divided kingdom having the toughness of iron but also the weakness inherent in clay.

Daniel 2 further describes the feet or final form of the

last empire as a brittle kingdom illustrated by the fact that iron and clay do not adhere to one another. The text specifies that the iron and clay will combine in the *"seed of men"*. This phrase has been much debated but most commentators agree that it alludes to political alliances based on inter-marriage.[29] Such intermarrying long characterized the harem of the Sultan who almost exclusively married foreign women. In a similar way many Islamic radicals in our day are adept at enlisting or forcing foreign women to marry them and bear them children.

Put together, the Revelation and Daniel's prophecies, despite being written centuries apart, paint a stunningly coherent picture. When we allow the evidence to lead they way, the scene of humankind's final 'crime' scene comes alive. Before moving on to other corollary passages, let's take a moment see the picture so far.

World Empires	Daniel 2 - Statue	Daniel 7 - Beasts	Revelation 17 - Heads
Egypt and Assyria			1st-2nd Head
Babylon	Golden Head	Lion	3rd Head
Medo-Persia	Silver Chest & Arms	Bear	4th Head
Greco-Roman	Bronze Thighs	Leopard	5th-6th Head
Islamic-Ottoman	Iron Legs	Dreadful Beast	7th Head
10 Kings-antichrist	Iron & Clay Feet/10 Toes	10 horns - Little Horn	10 Horns - 8th Ruler

The King Of The North

In our search to gather clues about the identity of the antichrist we have seen already that he will be a boastful and violent world leader. His kingdom will likely be rooted in a revived Islamic/Ottoman Empire from which he will rise to power on the shoulders of a 10 King coalition, three of whom he will depose when he establishes himself as their supreme leader. To gain more insight into his character we now turn to Daniel 11 which paints a striking picture of the antichrist's persona and dominion.

The majority of chapter 11 is a breath-taking account of the historic struggle that took place between the Ptolemaic Empire which ruled what is modern-day Egypt and the Seleucid Empire which was based in what is today eastern Turkey. After the sweeping conquest of Alexander the Great his empire was divided between four of his generals, two of whom were Ptolemy and Seleucus. Over time, their royal descendants became the dominant powers in the Middle East. This chapter describes in tremendous detail their tumultuous rivalry focusing especially on Antiochus Epiphanes (11:21-35). He was particularly note-worthy for his tyranny of the Jewish people and for defiling the temple in Jerusalem by setting up 'the abomination of desolation.' Interestingly, he is also described in Daniel 8 as a 'small horn' akin to the antichrist. Because of this most commentators agree that Antiochus Epiphanes was in fact a prophetic fore-shadowing or prototype of the yet future world leader who will likewise persecute the Jewish people and defile their temple.

Towards the end of verse 35, the narrative regarding the Maccabean revolt of the second century B.C. comes to a close with a reference to the 'end time.' Then, in the next verse, Daniel takes a giant leap forward to the end times and begins to describe the actions of someone most believe to be the antichrist. Again, the fact that this comes on the heels of the description of his prototype Antiochus Epiphanes, the ruler of the northern Seleucid Empire suggests a deeper connection.

And the king shall do as he wills. He shall exalt himself and magnify himself above every god, and shall speak astonishing things against the God of gods. He shall prosper till the indignation is accomplished; for what is decreed shall be done. He shall pay no attention to the gods of his fathers, or to the one beloved by women. He shall not pay attention to any other god, for he shall magnify himself above all. He shall honor the god of fortresses instead of these. A god whom his fathers did not know he shall honor with gold and silver, with precious stones and costly gifts. He shall deal with the strongest fortresses with the help of a foreign god. Those who acknowledge him he shall load with honor. He shall make them rulers over many and shall divide the land for a price. At the time of the end, the king of the south shall attack him, but the king of the north shall rush upon him like a whirlwind, with chariots and horsemen, and with many ships. And he shall come into countries and shall overflow and pass through. He shall come into the glorious land. And tens of thousands shall fall, but these shall be delivered out of his hand: Edom and Moab and the main part of the Ammonites. He shall stretch out his hand against the countries, and the land of Egypt shall not escape. He shall become ruler of the treasures of gold and of silver, and all the precious things of Egypt, and the Libyans and the Cushites shall follow in his train. But news from the east and the north shall alarm him, and he shall go out with great fury to destroy and devote many to destruction. And he shall pitch his palatial tents between the sea and the glorious holy mountain. Yet he shall come to his end, with none to help him (Daniel 11:36-45).

These verses describe the antichrist as the king who does what he wills. In this he is very much like his prototype Antiochus; he blasphemes God, desecrates the sacred and even magnifies himself as a kind of god. He takes great pride in amassing treasures, conquering new lands and dividing the spoils with his followers. In this he is further reminiscent of many a political leader and prophet who has risen in the Middle East.

Then in verse 40 the text describes how the 'King of

the South' collides with him. Then the 'King of the North' is said to storm against the king of the south. This reference harks back to the ancient rivalry between the Ptolemies and Seleucids described earlier in the chapter. Because the antichrist is foreshadowed by Antiochus Epiphanes, i.e. the king of the north, it seems only logical to equate the antichrist with the aforementioned 'King of the North.' Such a reading of the text links the antichrist to the ancient empire of the Seleucids to the north of Israel in modern day Turkey, Iraq and Syria.

The rest of the chapter describes the Anti-Christ as he storms against Egypt, being helped interestingly by the Libyans and Cushites (peoples south of Egypt). Finally rumors from the east and north compel him to turn back to the land of Israel with vengeful intent. In anticipation of some great war, likely the war of armageddon, he pitches his royal tents between the Mediterranean Sea and the glorious holy mountain, namely Zion. But his end is decreed and he will be completely destroyed.

The final chapter of Daniel goes on to describe this period as a time of great distress for the nation of Israel. The angel Gabriel gives Daniel details that can only refer to the great tribulation spoken of earlier. All of this confirms that the 'King of the North' described just previous is in fact the antichrist, the final adversary of Jesus Christ.

For the sake of our study on the antichrist, this passage not only outlines his final military maneuvers but it further describes his character as an arrogant despot. Furthermore it points us to the ancient lands of the Seleucid Empire to the north of Israel as the likely location for his future kingdom.

Gog And Magog

Another Biblical passage that seems to point to the north of Israel as the potential seat of power for the future antichrist's kingdom is Ezekiel 38-39. The prophet Ezekiel, in the famous 'valley of dead bones' vision of chapter 37, after describing the final reconstitution and spiritual restoration of the nation of Israel in correlation with the fulfillment of the New Covenant, then turns to describe a final invasion of Israel by an enemy coalition led by one called Gog. While the etymology of his name has no clear precedent in Scripture, what is clear is that he masterminds a great attack on God's people in the end times.

Son of man, set your face toward Gog, of the land of Magog, the chief prince of Meshech and Tubal, and prophesy against him and say, Thus says the Lord GOD: Behold, I am against you, O Gog, chief prince of Meshech and Tubal. And I will turn you about and put hooks into your jaws, and I will bring you out, and all your army, horses and horsemen, all of them clothed in full armor, a great host, all of them with buckler and shield, wielding swords. Persia, Cush, and Put are with them, all of them with shield and helmet; Gomer and all his hordes; Beth-togarmah from the uttermost parts of the north with all his hordes—many peoples are with you (Ezekiel 38:2-6).

In the following verses Gog and his hordes storm into the land of Israel with every intention of sweeping it into the sea. However, God keeps emphasizing that he is in fact the one drawing them into a trap 'in the latter years,' in order to destroy them in his judgment. Ezekiel notes that they come from their place 'out of the uttermost parts of the north' together with many peoples, a great host intent on destroying Israel.

The rest of chapter 38 and 39, goes on to detail a great earthquake and various cataclysmic events all reminiscent of the final judgments leading up to the great battle of armageddon (Revelation 16). In the end these 'northern' armies are destroyed by God's judgments and their corpses are fed to the birds, just as depicted in Revelation 19. With all these details lining up so well it seems evident that the same event is being described, namely the final military conflagration of the great tribulation.

When it comes to ascertaining the identity of this army, from the outset their marauding leader is described as a prince being from the land of Magog and the chief prince of Meshech and Tubal. Now some translations like the NASB, have 'Rosh' listed here as a separate nation and some interpreters have attempted to associate this with Russia. However elsewhere in the Scriptures "Rosh" is consistently used in its straight forward meaning "head or chief" as translated in the ESV.[30] As we read on down the passage the text describes other nations that are joined to Gog in his efforts to destroy Israel, these include, Persia, Cush, Put, Gomer and Beth-Togarmah. Of course most of these names are not in use today as Ezekiel was listing the names of nations and people groups in his day (approx. 600 B.C.). However in seeking to correlate them to the 'latter days' we can try to identify the geographic location of the people in Ezekiel's day and match it to nations that are there today. In this way the identification of these peoples are pretty straight-forward.

- Persia is modern Iran. This is the easiest to pin down because Iranians still refer to themselves as Persians.
- Cush is known to be the area south of Egypt and includes Sudan, Somalia and/or Ethiopia
- Lut is historically a reference to Libya in North Africa west of Egypt.
- Gomer is a bit more difficult to pinpoint but is historically linked to the ancient Cimmerians living in northern Turkey.[31]
- Beth-togarmah literally means "the house of Togarmah". Interestingly to this day the Turkish republics of central Asia (Turkmenistan, Tajikistan and others) consider themselves the children of their ancestor Togarmah.

Now the more important question related to our study of the antichrist focuses on the identification of Magog, Meshech and Tubal, the lands that he governs. First we must note that Gog is described as being from the land of Magog and also being the chief prince of Meshech and Tubal. Thus these lands are clearly related. We first come across these names in Genesis 10:2

as it describes the sons of Japheth. In ancient times, these settled across the northern segment of the Middle East.

Historically the lands in question, Tubal and Meshech in particular, have been associated with the geographic region of Anatolia in central Turkey. Meshech is known in history as the Muski who often fought with the Assyrians to the east.[32] Tubal was a close trading partner and ally of Meshech. Both of these names appear in Ezekiel 27:13 as trading partners of Tyre in modern Lebanon.

The reference to Magog is more difficult to pin down but most scholars place it somewhere in eastern Turkey. Josephus identified them with the Scythians, a tribe renowned for their fighting.[33] Interestingly some ancient Islamic traditions likewise refer to the Turks in particular as Gog and Magog, because they migrated to the region of the Middle East from the far east. Although we may not be able to establish exact relationships between these names and current places and peoples, it seems clear that we are speaking of the northern segment of the Middle East in general and most likely the geographical region held today by the republic of Turkey and Syria in particular.[34]

As we noted, this seven nation coalition led by Gog and his nation Magog, will seek to wipe Israel off the map. Now, exactly when this great northern invasion will take place is a matter of much discussion. First of all we must note that the only other mention of Gog and Magog is in Revelation 20:8, which is clearly after the millennial reign of Christ. There, the name describes the armies mustered by Satan in his final revolt against Christ's earthly kingdom. Ezekiel 38-39 however seem to describe an invasion prior to Christ's return, nearing the end of the tribulation, as the revelation of the future Messianic Temple comes afterwards (Ezekiel 40-48) The fact that the only other reference to Gog and Magog, relates to the final rebellion at the end of the millennial reign has led many to see them as one event. However, it is better to see that last reference to Gog and Magog in the Revelation as highlighting the similarity of the final rebellion to the earlier battle of armageddon.

Thus is appears that Gog is another name for none other than the antichrist and Ezekiel 38 is thus a description of the final attack on God's people in Jerusalem detailed many times elsewhere (Zechariah 14). Once again if we look carefully at the modern nations listed as part of this anti-Semitic coalition we note that they all share the Islamic faith as a common denominator, a religion that has a long history of hatred towards God's people. Thus it would not be surprising that they would band together against Israel as they already pine for its destruction.

Another note of interest is that Daniel spoke of the antichrist removing three kings from the ten nation coalition that he initially leads. That would leave seven kingdoms, the same number of kingdoms listed by Ezekiel. In this regard Micah 5:5 is intriguing as it speaks of the future enemy of Israel as 'the Assyrian', namely from the north, coming with seven kings, himself being the eighth. Interestingly the nation of Egypt is not listed in this evil coalition. Could it be that at this time they will be experiencing the great revival predicted in Isaiah 19? Maybe this will be the reason why the antichrist attacks Egypt as detailed in the last portion of Daniel 11. The puzzle is coming together!

The Man Of Lawlessness

One final passage bearing upon the identity of the antichrist is found in Paul's letter to the Thessalonians. In his first letter Paul encouraged the relatively new believers in that Macedonian city to live in holiness even as the 'Day of the Lord' approaches. Soon afterwards it seems that they had received some message leading some to believe that the Lord's coming had already taken place and that they had missed the 'gathering' in the clouds described by Paul in his first letter. Thus the apostle writes to clarify this matter.

Now concerning the coming of our Lord Jesus Christ and our being gathered together to him, we ask you, brothers, not to be quickly shaken in mind or alarmed, either by a spirit or a spoken word, or a letter seeming to be from us, to the effect that the day of the Lord has come. Let no one deceive you in any way. For that day will not come, unless the rebellion comes first, and the man of lawlessness is revealed, the son of destruction, who opposes and exalts himself against every so-called god or object of worship, so that he takes his seat in the temple of God, proclaiming himself to be God. Do you not remember that when I was still with you I told you these things? And you know what is restraining him now so that he may be revealed in his time. For the mystery of lawlessness is already at work. Only he who now restrains it will do so until he is out of the way. And then the lawless one will be revealed, whom the Lord Jesus will kill with the breath of his mouth and bring to nothing by the appearance of his coming. The coming of the lawless one is by the activity of Satan with all power and false signs and wonders, and with all wicked deception for those who are perishing, because they refused to love the truth and so be saved (2 Thessalonians 2:1-10).

As Paul begins his discussion it is important to note that he links three important eschatological events into one: The coming of Christ, the gathering of believers and the day of the Lord. He seems to see these not as distinct events but as intimately related and potentially contemporaneous. More on this in the chapter on the rapture.

Paul goes on to comfort the Thessalonians with the news that they have not missed anything yet. He then synthesizes all the signs leading to the second coming into two main ones: The Apostasy and the Antichrist. Jesus spoke at great length about the apostasy that would be a harbinger of the end times. In other passages Paul also speaks to the many trials that will accompany the last days (1 Timothy 4:1-3; 2 Timothy 3:1-9, 4:3-4). It is not hard to see some of these disturbing predictions already being fulfilled in our own day and age.

In 2 Thessalonians, however, Paul takes time to outline his understanding of the antichrist. The very fact that he expends all this effort to explain the antichrist to New Testament believers, should give us reason to believe that the church may at least in part experience the events he is describing. The apostle prefers to call him 'the man of lawlessness' likely because he is described in Daniel 11 as one who flaunts God's laws and tries to establish his own. He is also the one who brings about the great 'abomination of desolation,' the ultimate desecration of the temple. Here Paul seems to be detailing that very event when he describes the antichrist entering the temple and taking his seat on the throne of God. That would indeed be the ultimate sacrilege!

Now exactly how this will take place is yet to be seen. First a temple needs to be rebuilt in Jerusalem something which will be a monumental achievement in its own right, if it doesn't spark World War III. We know from Daniel that in the middle of the antichrist's seven year covenant he will somehow desecrate the temple. Indeed taking his seat in the place of God all the while claiming to be divine would indeed qualify as a great abomination especially to the Jewish people. Other events will certainly accompany this sacrilege including putting a stop to sacrifices on the temple altar and setting up a pagan statue of himself. Ultimately, before the end, the temple will be demolished again just as Jesus predicted in the Olivet Discourse.

Paul goes on to remind the Thessalonians that they had discussed this previously. In other words, it seems like it was a priority for Paul to have these discussions even with new believers. Then Paul says something that still mystifies many today: "*You know what is restraining him now so that he may be revealed in his time.*" Evidently the believers then knew exactly what he was talking about whereas we are largely clueless. What could it be that hinders the revelation of the antichrist and ultimately stands in the way of the unfolding of this final period of history?

Of all the eschatological conundrums this one has proven one of the most elusive to interpreters down through the centuries. Many suggestions have been made including the Roman Empire[35] and the Holy Spirit.[36] Those that hold a pre-tribulation rapture position often interpret this in relation to the removal of the church from the earth prior to the seven year of tribulation, thus paving the way for the unmitigated spread of lawlessness. A careful look at the text shows that the restrainer (Gk: Katekon) is used twice, once in neuter form and the second time in masculine form. Those who interpret the restrainer as the Holy Spirit like to seize on this as evidence for their view, since the third person of the Trinity is often referred to in the neuter. However, the second reference the restrainer also says that it will be taken away to allow for the antichrist's unmitigated reign on earth. Do we really want to claim that there will be a time in human history when the Holy Spirit will not be actively present on earth? That is a frightening proposition.

So who could fit the role of the restrainer? He is clearly some supernatural agent who is actively holding back the full expression of satanic lawlessness, who, at some point, will eventually step aside allowing the final form of the antichrist's government to be established. This has led some interpreters to suggest an angelic figure, more specifically, the archangel Michael, as a candidate for this extraordinary role. Support for this view is found in the obvious linkage between Paul's description of the antichrist and Daniel's description of the same in Daniel 9-12. There Michael is described as the divine *restrainer* of satanic powers behind the great world empires (Daniel 10:13-21). Then in Daniel 12:1 we read, *"At that time **shall arise** Michael, the great prince who has charge of your people. And there shall be a time of trouble, such as never has been since there was a nation till that time."*

In this last passage, Michael the archangel is portrayed as the great defender of Israel, and yet, the Jewish nation is here plunged into the great tribulation. How could that be? It has been suggested that the verb describing Michael as 'arising' can also mean to 'step aside' as evidenced in the LXX.[37] Thus Michael would actually be removing his protective influence and allowing Israel to suffer the unprecedented rigors of the end times' tribulation. Could it be that Paul's 'restrainer' refers to Michael and the heavenly hosts who will be commanded to 'stand down' and allow Satan and the antichrist to have free rein in the great tribulation? Later in our study of the Revelation we will learn more about Michael's role in the end times.

Paul further notes that the mystery of lawlessness, or the spirit of the antichrist, as John calls it, has been at work all along (1 John 2:18, 4:3). However Satan's plans have been hindered from coming into full force because of God's great mercy in waiting for more to come to repentance and his angelic armies stemming the tide of evil. Scripture is clear that we are caught in the cross-hairs of a cosmic spiritual battle between evil and good (Ephesians 6:10-12). However, as we enter the final stage of human history, it seems evident that God will have his forces of light stand down which will finally allow the devil free rein to deceive the nations and wreak havoc on earth. In fact his surrogates, the antichrist and the false prophet, will even be allowed to work miracles in order to ultimately delude the masses into following them to their eventual destruction. This will take place until the day the Lord Jesus appears again with his angels and slays them with the breath of his mouth (Matthew 24:30-31; Revelation 19:11-21).

> ...when the Lord Jesus is revealed from heaven with his mighty angels in flaming fire, inflicting vengeance on those who do not know God and on those who do not obey the gospel of our Lord Jesus. They will suffer the punishment of eternal destruction, away from the presence of the Lord and from the glory of his might, when he comes on that day to be glorified in his saints, and to be marveled at among all who have believed, because our testimony to you was believed (2 Thessalonians 1:7b-10).

Conclusion

The Bible is clear that no human government will ever be able to endure. Nonetheless, many modern Christians have fallen for the lie that democracy is somehow sacred; the ultimate form of civilization and the perfect prescription for global governance. When compared to despotic dictators and maniacal monarchs, democracy does seem much more benign, and yet, when we take stock of the today's democratic world order, we can see that it has failed not just in the Middle East but even in the West. This is because rule by the people for the people will ultimately fall prey to the tyranny of the same people.

William Golding's novel 'Lord of the Flies' written in 1954, in many ways epitomized this tragic truth. In his story a group of teenagers find themselves marooned on an island after their plane crashes. Being somewhat educated, they decide to pursue a democratic form of governance but before long inter-personal power struggles tear the group apart. Soon the motley group spirals into utter depravity as they begin attacking each other like wild animals. Does this sound familiar?

Down through history we have seen this same narrative play out over and over. Every new kingdom or republic has promised peace and prosperity for its constituents. However, sooner or later, the gangrene of human depravity sets in and the whole enterprise comes crashing down, usually subjugated by the next kingdom which claims it will make everything right. Thus the cycle continues and we should not expect democracy to be any different. Even now we can see how the freedoms enshrined in the U.S. Bill of Rights are being turned on their head and used to legitimize and even legislate all forms of immorality. The end of democracy is not far off. God forgive us for having put our faith in democracy and having lost sight of the only answer to all the world's problems, Jesus Christ.

As we approach the end, the Scriptures outline one last

and ultimately futile attempt by humankind to bring order to the chaos. From what we have learned it is clear that this final human kingdom will be rooted in the Middle East, where all the ancient empires resided. It will evidently be founded on some coalition of ten kings or princes and their respective kingdoms. One great leader will arise who will succeed in capturing the imagination of these regional rulers and will eventually rise to lead them all. This 'prince' will evidently hail from the northern lands of Israel boasting authority over a broad coalition of Middle Eastern nations.

Eventually this powerful and likely charismatic leader will succeed in orchestrating some great treaty between the Middle Eastern nations and Israel. This will involve a rebuilding of the historic temple complex in Jerusalem, which will likely incorporate the Islamic beliefs of its neighbors as well (Revelation 11:2). Such a 'peace agreement' will surely be hailed as a huge success and will likely earn him the Nobel Peace prize. Finally someone will appear to have solved the Middle East dilemma. This will initiate the beginning of the final seven years leading ultimately to the return of Christ.

Soon after this historic agreement is brokered, all the promises of peace will begin to unravel as God begins to pour out his judgments in which wars, famine and death will stalk humanity. The great peace treaty will also prove to be a sham as it will soon fall apart when, at the mid-point of the seven years' treaty, the coming 'prince', the antichrist, desecrates the temple by claiming to be some form of deity. This will send the Jewish people into a frenzy but will also hasten their repentance and ultimate restoration. Ironically, this final phase of human history will be characterized by both great persecution and global revival. It will indeed be the 'the best of times and the worst of times.'

As the end of the seven years draws to an end the 'King of the North', the antichrist, will muster all his armies to attack a rebellious Egypt which evidently stands in opposition to his cause. During this time three of the 10 kings will fall as the leading prince consolidates power and leads the charge. After subjugating Egypt the antichrist will direct all his wrath towards Jerusalem. He will call on all nations to join him in attacking Israel. This will set the stage for the final battle of armageddon. In the end however, it will be Jesus who will have the final word when he appears in the clouds and later descends to take on the enemies of Israel.

At this point many readers are craving to know who I think the antichrist will be. Let me be forthright in saying that I don't believe we can ascertain his identity until he arrives on the scene. For example, much effort has been put in to calculating the number of the beast, 666. However, the fact that it is called the number of his name, means that we cannot calculate it until we know his name (Revelation 13:18). As noted before, the Bible gives us a roadmap for the future but we cannot make positive identifications until we get there. However, if we know what to expect, then we will not be caught by surprise.

Based on the specifications and rough outline provided by the prophets, we can be fairly certain that the Middle East will be the epicenter of this final conflagration. Furthermore all indications point to the north of Israel, the ancient lands of the Seleucids, as the origin of this end times' beast. In this regard I have mentioned Turkey and other nations in the Middle East. Frankly, I mention these with great sadness, because I love the peoples of the Middle East and Turkey in particular. In fact, my family and I have spent our lifetimes trying to share the gospel of Jesus Christ with the peoples of this region. So let me be clear in stating that I have no vendetta against Turkey or any Muslim country. As a Bible teacher I am simply trying to be faithful to the Scriptures and where it points me with regard to the end times. If the end is indeed at hand, then it is likely that these nations will play key roles in fulfilling Biblical prophecy. However, if the Lord tarries, it is possible that the political makeup of the region may be different in the future. Either way, when it comes to the end times, it seems abundantly clear that we should keep our eyes riveted on the Middle East.

Some will certainly question my conclusion that the Beast will likely arise from the Middle East. Could the Islamic/ Ottoman Empire of yesteryear truly revive? As one who has lived in this region, I can testify to the radical changes that Turkey in particular has undergone since we arrived there in 2001. What was once a staunchly secular country preparing to join the European Union, is now posturing as the rejuvenated champion of Islam across the region. In this unexpected transformation, not only have they lost many western friends, they have also made themselves the chief antagonist of Israel in the region. All of this seems to be paving the way for the rise of the Beast.

Most westerners are not familiar with Islamic eschatology but a short summary here will help to show how it might indeed fit hand in glove with the Biblical framework. Muslims also believe the end will come soon in which Islam will be reinstated as the head of all nations. Although different interpretations of the details abound, most believe that one called 'Mahdi', the rightly guided one, will appear in the end times to restore the fortunes of the humiliated Muslim 'ummah' or commonwealth. He will be aided by the return of the prophet Isa (Jesus), who will lend his support to the Mahdi by working miracles. They will in turn assemble the Muslim nations and urge them to make a lying covenant with Israel. In the end however they will betray their word and attack Israel. They will especially seek the destruction of Islam's version of the antichrist, which they called 'Dajjal.' He is described as a one-eyed Jew who claims to be God incarnate and fights for Israel. Their eschatology teaches that this impostor, the Dajjal, and his people the Jews will be finally destroyed by Isa and the Mahdi thus paving the way for a global Islamic Golden Age.[38]

It is not hard to see how the eschatological expectations of Muslims today could be serendipitously fulfilled by the events prophesied in Scriptures. The 'mirror effect' is too uncanny to be coincidental. In fact since the demise of the Islamic/ Ottoman Empire one hundred years ago, Muslims worldwide have been dreaming of their glorious restoration to power. It is this eschatological vision of a renewed caliphate that spurred Muslim faithful from around the globe to join Al-Qaida in Afghanistan and later ISIS in Syria. The same promise of global domination continues to galvanize Muslims around the world and inspires new attempts at reestablishing the caliphate lost in 1923.

The script is written and the stage is set. Now we await the actors. It would not take much for a magnetic Muslim leader claiming to be 'Mahdi', supported by a miracle working 'Isa', to bring the divided Muslim nations together creating a global superpower. Whether or not this will happen and would ultimately prove to be the fulfillment of the Biblical prophecies is yet to be seen. For now we watch and pray, doing all in our power to save more people from impending destruction while there is still time.

6. THE RAPTURE

Those who love the Lord's return are champing at the bit by now, wondering when we will get to that part we all love to argue about the most, namely the rapture. Indeed, the subject of the rapture, as presented by classic Christian movies like A Thief in the Night and later Left Behind, has mesmerized generations of believers. Ever since my childhood I was especially impacted by these. In fact the fear of being 'left behind' played a significant role in my choice to trust in Christ at a young age. Since then however, I have learned that the timing of the rapture, far from being set in stone, is in fact a hotly debated matter. In fact, among eschatological topics, no subject elicits as much reaction as differing opinions on the rapture.

Ten years ago, when I sat down to write my book on eschatology in Turkish, I was especially looking forward to elaborating this section. I had always held and taught a pre-tribulation rapture position, namely that Christ would return secretly to rapture the church before the seven year tribulation got underway, thus sparing us from his wrath. However, as I got started writing out my usual arguments and explanations of classic proof texts I suddenly began to realize that these verses were not really offering ironclad support for my preferred view. After some frustrating attempts, I had to scrap what I had written and go back to the drawing board. I soon came to the realization that my pre-tribulation position was not predicated so much on Scripture as it was on my insistence of keeping Israel and the church entirely separate. At the same time I was also beginning to realize that such a rigid distinction was Biblically untenable.

Other traditional arguments I had always put forward related to the church being spared God's wrath, and yet many passages describing the tribulation were actually penned to the churches. Why would God reveal all the details of the tribulation to the church, when she will not even have to endure it? I also liked to highlight major differences between the rapture and the second coming of Christ. However, the more I studied the relevant passages the more they seemed to coalesce and converge. Finally, based on 1 Corinthians 15:51, I used to be convinced that the rapture was some kind of mystery appearing. And yet, upon closer examination, I had to recognize that the mystery related not to the timing of the rapture but to the fact that some would indeed be taken to heaven alive and transformed in an instant along with all the other believers being resurrected from the dead.

Although immensely disappointing and frustrating initially, realizing the flimsiness of my arguments forced me to reevaluate my position and follow the Biblical compass instead. With time I came to recognize my infatuation with the rapture as rather self-serving. I was really taking great pains to ensure that I was would not be around to suffer the great tribulation, when the Bible in fact repeatedly calls us to suffer much for Christ. Having lived in the Middle East for the last two decades, I have gained a new appreciation for the mysterious joy and peace that comes with joining the rest of the global church as they more than often have to suffer much for the sake of Christ.

Ironically, the fact that the western church can afford to spend so much time and energy in discussing this subject began to seem rather self indulgent. This was especially driven home to me when I realized that there are really just a handful of verses that can be legitimately linked to the rapture, while on the other hand, there are hundreds of verses detailing the second coming. From a Biblical perspective the real headline of the future is not our deliverance but Christ's glorious return. In fact, the subject of the rapture is a mere footnote in the larger context of Biblical eschatology. And yet believers in the West are willing to verbally chastise each other and even break fellowship over the subject. On the contrary, among believers in the Middle East, it is hardly a hot-button topic as we have much greater issues to deal with, including ongoing persecution.

Now, none of this is to say that the rapture is not important or unbiblical. Rather we must put it back into the Biblical context and let the exegetical evidence lead the way not our own presuppositions. I do not intend to offend or chastise my many pre-tribulation friends here. On the contrary, I have found that my 'dispensational' pre-millennial upbringing has served me well in teaching me to take Bible exegesis seriously. Neither will I jump on a mid or post-tribulation bandwagon. My only hope is to urge us all to take another long and hard look at the relevant passages and hold our position in this regard more lightly even as we wait to see how it will indeed all come together.

The Central Passage

There are only a few passages that speak directly to the fact that Christ will return to retrieve those who love him (John 14:3). Some of these speak more specifically to the necessary transformation our physical bodies will undergo in order to live in the presence of Christ (1 Corinthians 15:50-53; Philippians 3:21). Others to the fact that his return will indeed catch believers by surprise (Luke 12:35-40; Revelation 22:7). Most other passages usually brought into this discussion relate to the future coming of Christ in general, namely, the main event (Revelation 1:7). However, regarding the subject of the rapture, the passage that really serves as the epicenter for this topic is 1 Thessalonians 4-5. Let's read the relevant verses in their entirety:

But we do not want you to be uninformed, brothers, about those who are asleep, that you may not grieve as others do who have no hope. For since we believe that Jesus died and rose again, even so, through Jesus, God will bring with him those who have fallen asleep. For this we declare to you by a word from the Lord, that we who are alive, who are left until the coming of the Lord, will not precede those who have fallen asleep. For the Lord himself will descend from heaven with a cry of command, with the voice of an archangel, and with the sound of the trumpet of God. And the dead in Christ will rise first. Then we who are alive, who are left, will be caught up together with them in the clouds to meet the Lord in the air, and so we will always be with the Lord. Therefore encourage one another with these words. Now concerning the times and the seasons, brothers, you have no need to have anything written to you. For you yourselves are fully aware that the day of the Lord will come like a thief in the night. While people are saying, "There is peace and security," then sudden destruction will come upon them as labor pains come upon a pregnant woman, and they will not escape. But you are not in darkness, brothers, for that day to surprise you like a thief. For you are all children of light, children of the day. We are not of the night or of the darkness. So then let us not sleep, as others do, but let us keep awake and be sober. For those who sleep, sleep at night, and those who get drunk, are drunk at night. But since we belong to the day, let us be sober, having put on the breastplate of faith and love, and for a helmet the hope of salvation. For God has not destined us for wrath, but to obtain salvation through our Lord Jesus Christ, who died for us so that whether we are awake or asleep we might live with him. Therefore encourage one another and build one another up, just as you are doing (1 Thessalonians 4:13-5:11).

Despite being newly established, the church fellowship in Thessalonica had clearly received some teaching from Paul on the Lord's coming. This is because, as noted earlier, the subject of our blessed hope is an integral part of the gospel. However, from the verses above, it is evident that some of the believers of this group had recently passed away, maybe because of persecution. It seems this had caused some consternation in the fellowship as they likely expected Christ to return soon, before any of them had to suffer death. Paul however urges them not to fret and to remember that the future resurrection of their loved ones is guaranteed by the resurrection of the Lord Jesus. He further implies that their spirits are already 'with him', and that their bodies are really just 'sleeping' until the time of Christ's return when they will be resurrected.

Paul goes on to give the most detailed description of the rapture in Scriptures. However, it is important to note at the outset that he anchors this in *"a word from the Lord."*   Where else in the Bible is there a detailed description of the rapture? Nowhere in the Old Testament to be sure. However when we compare this passage with the Olivet Discourse in Matthew 24 where the Lord Jesus speaks of his second coming, we will find many elements that line up almost perfectly with what Paul is describing here. Thus, from the outset, the apostle Paul seems to be linking his statements on the rapture to the Olivet Discourse of Jesus thus implying that they refer to one and the same event.

Paul's first point is that the dead will not be forgotten. In fact, when Christ returns, their bodies will be resurrected and rejoined with their spirits in heaven even as those who are alive are raptured and similarly transformed in order to join them in the presence of the Lord Jesus. Thus, whether we are alive or deceased at Christ's return, it will make no difference, we will all be reunited in his glorious presence instantaneously.

Then Paul begins to relay some of the details of Christ's coming. First he notes that it will really truly be the Lord Jesus Christ who will descend in human form, not some spirit or phantom. Indeed we believe in the corporal return of Christ, namely that he will return in the same way that he left (Acts 1:11). Secondly, he notes three seemingly important signs that will accompany the rapture: A cry of command, the voice of the archangel and the trumpet of God. Upon closer scrutiny each of these has a close parallel in passages relating to the second coming.

Of these signs, the cry of command is likely the most difficult to place in Scriptures. What is he referencing here? He seems to be taking us back to the prophet Joel who spoke in great detail of the yet future day of the Lord. The prophet Joel specifically noted that even as Israel was being swamped by the invading 'northern army' the Lord would appear to them and cry out at that time:

> The LORD utters his voice before his army, for his camp is exceedingly great; he who executes his word is powerful. For the day of the LORD is great and very awesome; who can endure it? Return to the Lord "Yet even now," declares the LORD, "return to me with all your heart, with fasting, with weeping, and with mourning; and rend your hearts and not your garments." (Joel 2:11-13b).

The Lord's cry at that time is to all who will hear but especially to his rebellious people Israel, who must repent in order for him to sit on the throne of David. Thus he pleads with them to finally repent and open the way for his return. In the following chapter we further read of God roaring like a lion over Israel (Joel 3:16).

This leads us to the second sign, the voice of the archangel. We know very little about such divine creatures except for the fact that Israel is guarded by one such angelic warrior named Michael. The prophet Daniel describes this mighty archangel as the great defender of Israel (Daniel 10:21, 12:1-2). We come across Michael again in Revelation 12 as he leads the heavenly hosts against Satan and his demons. At that time the angelic armies take charge of the 'heavens' banishing the devil and his cronies to the earth. It is likely that Michael is also the great angel that appears in Revelation 10 swearing 'by him who lives forever and ever, who created heaven and what is in it, *the earth and what is in it, and the sea and what is in it, that there would be no more delay but that in the days of the trumpet call to be sounded by the seventh angel, the mystery of God would be fulfilled, just as he announced to his servants the prophets.'* (Revelation 10:6-7). The fact that he ties his imperial declaration to the final trumpet about to sound makes the linkage even more compelling.

The third sign of the rapture according to 1 Thessalonians 4 is the blowing of the trumpet of God. In the Old Testament trumpets were blown to gather God's people to meetings or feasts, but also to prepare them for war. There are many other references to the final trumpet in the context of the last days. Most significantly it harks back to the trumpet mentioned in Jesus' end time discourse in Matthew 24:31: *"And he will send out his angels with a loud trumpet call, and they will gather his elect from the four winds, from one end of heaven to the other."* Christ's description of the angels gathering the believers from around the world sounds very much like the gathering together of believers described by the apostle Paul (2 Thessalonians 2:1).

In the parallel rapture passage of 1 Corinthians 15:52, Paul also links the resurrection of believers to the 'last trumpet.' The specification of this trumpet as the 'last' one, suggests that it is part of a series of trumpet blasts. When we turn to the Revelation we are introduced to seven angels blowing seven trumpets which herald the coming of God's final judgments (Revelation 8). The last trumpet however is singled out as bringing God's mystery to fulfillment. This harks back to the mystery of Christ's appearing and our glorious resurrection. When the final trumpet is sounded, this evokes the heavenly chorus: *"The kingdom of the world has become the kingdom of our Lord and of his Christ, and he shall reign forever and ever"* (Revelation 11:15). This sets into motion the final series of judgments represented by the seven bowls, including the battle of armageddon, culminating in the final descent of Christ.

What we have seen so far is that all the essential details

related to the rapture and resurrection of believers mentioned by Paul, tie in closely with Christ's description of his second coming. The linkage is further highlighted in the subsequent description of the 'Day of the Lord' in 1 Thessalonians 5.

The Day Of The Lord

After such an exhilarating description of our final reunion with Christ, the natural question is 'When will it take place?' Knowing this, Paul begins chapter five saying, *"Now concerning the times and the seasons, brothers, you have no need to have anything written to you..."* At the outset we might be disappointed that Paul refuses to answer the very question we are longing to decipher. However, Paul is simply restating Jesus' comments in Matthew 24:36 in which the Lord himself said it is impossible for anyone to know the time of his return. Once again the linkage is further strengthened when he speaks of the Christ's return as a 'thief in the night' (Matthew 24:42-44). More importantly the fact that Paul frames the context of the rapture in the larger Biblical category of the 'Day of the Lord' is very significant.

The subject of the 'Day of the Lord' takes us back to the Old Testament prophets who spoke at length about this phenomena. It is important to note that this phrase does not refer to one specific day in history, but rather to unique occasions when God intervenes in human affairs. Although this may sometimes relate to local and historic judgments of Israel's enemies, the phrase usually appears with reference to a yet future time in human history when the Lord will finally intervene to deliver his people, defeat Satan and establish his global reign. Although all of these events will come to a head on the day Christ physically returns to earth, the Biblical 'Day of the Lord' is also used more broadly to describe all the events surrounding this momentous occasion. In short, the 'Day of the Lord' is the epitome of God's judgment.

In order to appreciate the rich scriptural backdrop of this grand theme let us take some time to look at several prophetic passages that set the stage for it. As noted before, it is important to note that this phrase 'the Day of the Lord,' is sometimes used in reference to times in the past when God did judge Israel's enemies (Jeremiah 46:10; Ezekiel 30:3). These serve as examples of how God has not held back from judging his people's foes in the past and he certainly will not hesitate when the time comes in the future. For the purpose of our study we will focus on the passages that point to the yet future and final 'Day of the Lord.'

- Isaiah 13:9-11 - *Behold, **the day of the LORD** comes, cruel, with wrath and fierce anger, to make the land a desolation and to destroy its sinners from it. For the stars of the heavens and their constellations will not give their light; the sun will be dark at its rising, and the moon will not shed its light. I will punish the world for its evil, and the wicked for their iniquity; I will put an end to the pomp of the arrogant, and lay low the pompous pride of the ruthless.*

- Joel 2:1-11 - *Blow a trumpet in Zion; sound an alarm on my holy mountain! Let all the inhabitants of the land tremble, for the **day of the LORD** is coming; it is near, a day of darkness and gloom, a day of clouds and thick darkness! Like blackness there is spread upon the mountains a great and powerful people; their like has never been before, nor will be again after them through the years of all generations. Fire devours before them, and behind them a flame burns. The land is like the garden of Eden before them, but behind them a desolate wilderness, and nothing escapes them. Their appearance is like the appearance of horses, and like war horses they run. As with the rumbling of chariots, they leap on the tops of the mountains, like the crackling of a flame of fire devouring the stubble, like a powerful army drawn up for battle. Before them peoples are in anguish; all faces grow pale. Like warriors they charge; like soldiers they scale the wall. They march each on his way; they do not swerve from* their paths. They do not jostle one another; each marches in his path; they burst through the weapons and are not halted. They leap upon the city, they run upon the walls, they climb up into the houses, they enter through the windows like a thief. The earth quakes before them; the heavens tremble. The sun and the moon are darkened, and the stars withdraw their shining. The LORD utters his voice before his army, for his camp is exceedingly great; he who executes his word is powerful. For the **day of the LORD** is great and very awesome; who can endure it?

- Amos 5:18-24 - Woe to you who desire the **day of the LORD!** Why would you have the **day of the LORD?** It is darkness, and not light, as if a man fled from a lion, and a bear met him, or went into the house and leaned his hand against the wall, and a serpent bit him. Is not the **day of the LORD** darkness, and not light, and gloom with no brightness in it? "I hate, I despise your feasts, and I take no delight in your solemn assemblies. Even though you offer me your burnt offerings and grain offerings, I will not accept them; and the peace offerings of your fattened animals, I will not look upon them. Take away from me the noise of your songs; to the melody of your harps I will not listen. But let justice roll down like waters, and righteousness like an ever-flowing stream.

- Zephaniah 1:14-18 - The great **day of the LORD** is near, near and hastening fast; the sound of the **day of the LORD** is bitter; the mighty man cries aloud there. A day of wrath is that day, a day of distress and anguish, a day of ruin and devastation, a day of darkness and gloom, a day of clouds and thick darkness, a day of trumpet blast and battle cry against the fortified cities and against the lofty battlements. I will bring distress on mankind, so that they shall walk like the blind, because they have sinned against the LORD; their blood shall be poured out like dust, and their flesh like dung. Neither their silver nor their gold shall be able to deliver them on the **day of the wrath of the LORD.** In the fire of his jealousy, all the earth shall be consumed; for a full *and sudden end he will make of all the inhabitants of the earth.*

It is clear from these Old Testament prophecies that the 'Day of the Lord' is a euphemism for God's judgment. The Jews were tempted to see it only as a time when God would judge their enemies, and yet the Lord stresses that his judgment will not be partial to them. Furthermore, God's judgment of sinners is nothing to gloat about as it will be accompanied by all kinds of cataclysmic events which will devastate the whole planet. These descriptions clearly point to a yet future and final judgment of the whole world.

So when Paul mentions the 'Day of the Lord' in 1 Thessalonians 5, he is echoing this rich eschatological theme of judgment first voiced by the prophets. Elsewhere the apostle Peter also picks up this theme in his warnings regarding the final days saying, *"But the day of the Lord will come like a thief, and then the heavens will pass away with a roar, and the heavenly bodies will be burned up and dissolved, and the earth and the works that are done on it will be exposed"* (2 Peter 3:10). Thus, for Paul to speak of the day of the Lord is a clear reference to the second coming of Christ which will result in global judgment. This then links his teaching on the rapture to the final portion of the great tribulation.

Before leaving our discussion of the 'Day of the Lord,' it is noteworthy that in his second letter to the Thessalonians, Paul again mentions the 'Day of the Lord' in the context of Christ's return as follows: *"Now concerning the coming of our Lord Jesus Christ and our being gathered together to him, we ask you, brothers, not to be quickly shaken in mind or alarmed, either by a spirit or a spoken word, or a letter seeming to be from us, to the effect that the **day of the Lord** has come"* (2 Thessalonians 2:1-2). Here it is essential to note that Paul clearly links the 'coming of our Lord Jesus Christ' and 'our being gathered together to him,' i.e. the rapture. Then he places both of these in the context of the 'Day of the Lord.' In short, Paul doesn't seem to envisage the rapture as some separate event but rather as part and parcel of Christ's return in the day of the Lord.

God's Wrath

Returning to Paul's seminal explanation of the rapture in 1 Thessalonians 5, after anchoring it to the 'Day of the Lord,' Paul continues to describe those final days of human history in the same way Christ characterized them in the Olivet Discourse. Just as people are feeling good about themselves and promising peace and prosperity to each other, suddenly the world will be rocked by horrendous catastrophes. Jesus likened it to the days of Noah when people lived carefree not heeding God's warnings of impending judgment (Matthew 24:36-39). Elsewhere he further likened these final days to the grossly immoral times of Lot when men abandoned their natural desire for women and lusted after each other (Luke 17:26-30). So it will be in the final days, that human debauchery will plumb new depths eliciting divine judgment akin to that which rained down on Sodom and Gomorrah. Indeed God's judgment is not far off.

Another link that Paul makes to the Olivet discourse is evident in his mention of the 'labor pains.' This clearly harks back to Christ's characterization of the signs of the end times as 'labor pains' in Matthew 24, as discussed in great detail earlier.

Paul then urges the Thessalonian believers to be alert and awake as they await the coming of Christ. Some have pointed to this imminent aspect of the rapture as clearly distinguishing it from the second coming. However, once again we can see that Paul's statements here merely echo Jesus' warnings to his disciples given in the context of the second coming (Matthew 24:42-51). The Lord Jesus made it abundantly clear that his second coming would indeed catch many by surprise. This is because his parousia, as discussed earlier, is not a single event marking the last day of the seven year tribulation, but rather a chain of events, which will start with the sign of the Son of Man suddenly appearing in the heavens. It may take days if not months before the actual end of the campaign of armageddon and the final descent of Christ to earth. Thus his initial appearing and the gathering of the saints will indeed take place unexpectedly.

In his description of the rapture, again and again we have seen Paul reference the Lord Jesus' teaching on his second coming. Thus it seems best to envision the rapture not as a separate event but rather a starting point for a whole series of events culminating in Christ's arrival in Jerusalem. A comparison below of the rapture passages with Christ's description of his second coming will suffice to show the connections:

Rapture Discussion - 1 Thessalonians 4:13-5:11	Olivet Discourse - Matthew 24, Luke 21, Mark 13	Other Related Passages
Jesus descends with a loud voice of command	The Son of Man is seen coming on the clouds	Daniel 7:13; Joel 2:11-13
The voice of the archangel is heard	Jesus sends his angels out	Daniel 12:1; Revelation 10
The trumpet of God is heard	The angels blow the great trumpet	1 Corinthians 15:52; Revelation 11:15
The dead in Christ arise and are gathered to Jesus	The elect are gathered from around the globe	Daniel 12:2-3, 13; 1 Corinthians 15:23
No need to speak of the timing	No one knows the day or hour	Acts 1:7
In the context of the day of the Lord	Described as the day of the Lord's coming	Joel 2; 1 Corinthians 1:8; 2 Thessalonians 2:1-2
He will come like a thief in the night	Christ's return will be like a thief	2 Peter 3:10, Revelation 16:15
Prospects of peace followed by sudden destruction	People living carefree and immorally before judgment	Luke 17:26-30, Revelation 6:1-8
Destruction will come like sudden labor pains	The signs of the end will come like labor pains	Romans 8:19-22
Believers are called to be alert in light of Christ's sudden coming	The disciples are to be alert in light for Christ's sudden return	Matthew 25, 1 Peter 1:13

Returning to the final verses of Paul's discussion of the rapture, those who hold a pre-tribulation rapture position like to highlight the verse that states that God has not destined believers for wrath. To this they add other supporting verses like 1 Thessalonians 1:10 and Revelation 3:10. Thus they insist that the church will need to be raptured before the tribulation ensues. Indeed, the Bible is clear that the final judgments described by the prophets and outlined by the Revelation are targeting the ungodly (Romans 1:18, 2:5; Ephesians 5:6; Revelation 15). So how could believers be expected to suffer through the tribulation if God has promised to deliver us from the coming wrath?

First it must be noted that while believers are promised deliverance from God's final and eternal judgment, nowhere are believers exempted from the ongoing consequences of sin and death that continue to rack our world. In fact the Lord Jesus was explicit in saying that we would have tribulation in this world. All my pre-tribulation friends would surely agree that the very western notion and teaching that godly people should not expect to suffer any sickness or poverty is downright heretical. Not only does it belie so many clear teachings of Scripture but it also makes a mockery of believers around the world who suffer horribly for their faith in Christ. More than that it is a personal affront to the one who suffered unspeakable horrors for us on the cross, leaving us an example to follow in his footsteps (1 Peter 2:21-25).

Thus, it is important to stress here that belief in Christ does not insulate us from the world's problems or Satan's attacks. On the contrary, the Bible's teaching and my experience show that our continued faithfulness to God only make us a greater target to the enemy. Furthermore, the fact is that our own Scriptures were forged out of the fires of persecution, speaking more often than not to believers suffering the same fiery trial of their faith. Alas, the comforts of our modern times have made many lukewarm in their commitment to God's Word and his cause especially when it means suffering for Christ. In short, when it comes to suffering tribulation, the fact that believers have always suffered for Christ the world over gives us no guarantee that we will be completely exempted from the final period of tribulation.

When it comes to the tribulation and the outpouring of God's wrath upon mankind it is important to note when this will actually take place. As we will see in the next chapter on Revelation, the fullness of God's wrath will not be poured out on the earth, until the very end (Revelation 6:16-17, 14:10, 19:15). Consequently, by the time God's judgment is finally executed on mankind, believers will have indeed been taken up to the presence of the Lord Jesus. This however does not mean that we will not suffer greatly in those final years leading up to the end, just as believers the world over suffer for their faith today.

In summary, I agree with pre-tribulationists that based on God's Word we can expect to be suddenly delivered from the final form of God's wrath but I also believe that this will happen only after we have already endured much of the rigors of the tribulation. Again, instead of taking an 'either/or' approach to the rapture, I think we are wise to take the strengths of each view and combine them to form a more balanced perspective.

The Rapture In Revelation

One final argument posed by pre-tribulationalists, is an argument based on silence. They note that the Revelation does not make any mention of the church, except for the first three chapters, which are not prophetic in nature. From this they deduce that the church must be raptured previous to the tribulation and exempted from that whole period of judgment. While this may seem like a straight-forward deduction, any argument from silence is inherently hampered by the same.

A closer look at Revelation will show that during these final years of secular history God will not be silent. In fact it appears that there will be more people turning to Christ during this one troubled period than any other in our tragic history. Jesus himself made it clear that during this time the gospel of the kingdom would finally reach to the ends of the earth (Matthew 24:14). Of course it will also be a time of intense persecution as many are martyred for their faith in Christ, as evidenced by the saints gathered in heaven under the altar (Revelation 6:9-11). So if the church is not on earth during the tribulation who are these believers?

Chapter 7 of Revelation starts by introducing us to 144,000 Jewish believers from the tribes of Israel. While many have attempted to explain them away, they are obviously followers of the Messiah from Jewish descent (Revelation 14:1-5). Indeed any interpretation of this passage that simply whitewashes the many details provided by the apostle John, does a great injustice to the text and a disservice to the church. The rest of chapter 7 introduces us to a multitude of believers from every tribe and nation who have trusted in Christ as well, but have paid dearly for it. Upon inquiry John learns their identity: *"These are the ones coming out of the great tribulation. They have washed their robes and made them white in the blood of the Lamb"* (Revelation 7:14). Thus there are clearly believers from both Jewish and Gentile descent in the tribulation period.

Later in chapter 12 we are told of how Israel is forced to flee for her life during the great tribulation. At this time the dragon, Satan, persecutes God's people who in turn conquer him *"by the blood of the Lamb and by the word of their testimony, for they loved not their lives even unto death"* (Revelation 12:11). This chapter further speaks of Satan making war not only on the Jewish people but also on *"the rest of her offspring, on those who keep the commandments of God and hold to the testimony of Jesus"* (Revelation 12:17). This is a clear reference to Gentile believers. Thus the unmistakable picture emerges of both Jew and Gentile believers enduring great suffering at the hands of

Satan for their faith in Christ.

Also it is important to note that from the outset the whole of the Revelation was written to 'the churches' (Revelation 1:4). Throughout the first three chapters we keep coming upon this phrase: *"He who has an ear, let him hear what the Spirit says to the churches."* Now, it is clear that although Jesus is addressing specific complaints to particular church fellowships in Asia minor, his ultimate audience is the global church across the ages. This is driven home at the end of Revelation when he says *"I, Jesus, have sent my angel to testify to you about these things for the churches. I am the root and the descendant of David, the bright morning star"* (Revelation 22:16). So if the church is not expected to see any of the tribulation, why would the Lord go to so much trouble to outline in such vivid detail the events of that period in a book addressed to them?

Finally, some may be asking if the book of Revelation bears any hint of the rapture. I believe it provides more than a hint. In chapter 14 we find several pictures of God's people being reunited with Christ in glory. There is a unique reference to the Son of Man coming on the clouds harking back to Christ's Olivet Discourse, which alerts us to the significance of this great event,

> Then I looked, and behold, a white cloud, and seated on the cloud one like a son of man, with a golden crown on his head, and a sharp sickle in his hand. And another angel came out of the temple, calling with a loud voice to him who sat on the cloud, "Put in your sickle, and reap, for the hour to reap has come, for the harvest of the earth is fully ripe." So he who sat on the cloud swung his sickle across the earth, and the earth was reaped (Revelation 14:14-16).

Although some may question his identity, this seems to be a clear reference to the Son of Man, Jesus himself, as prophesied by Daniel 7. He is characterized as riding on the clouds or seated enthroned in the heavens. The fact that he has as *golden* crown points to his royal nature and ultimate victory.

This is no mere angel. He further carries a sickle with which he is urged to reap a glorious harvest of souls. This seems to be a clear allusion to Jesus' own description of the great harvest at the end of the age (Matthew 13:39). On the heels of this great harvest we have another angel sent to harvest, not the righteous but the wicked unto judgment. This leads quite literally to a blood-bath, namely the outcome of the battle of armageddon (Revelation 14:17-20).

The above passage highlighting the Son of Man seems to be a clear reference to the reaping of souls or rapture of believers during the tribulation. The timing according to the chronology of Revelation puts it toward the end of that period. Now, we might be surprised that it was not featured more prominently and yet this is because, as noted before, the rapture is not the main event. The return of Christ to vindicate God's eternal purposes and establish his reign is the real headline. Thus, we should not be surprised to find only a mere reference to the rapture tucked away in the Revelation.

Finally, the Revelation bears one more hint of the rapture, just in case we missed the first one. In Chapter 16, in the middle of a description of armageddon, where evil spirits are traversing the planet gathering volunteers, the Lord Jesus, who is dictating the Revelation, suddenly inserts a pertinent reminder to his followers: *"Behold, I am coming like a thief! Blessed is the one who stays awake, keeping his garments on, that he may not go about naked and be seen exposed!"* The reference to the 'thief in the night' is an unmistakable link both to the Olivet Discourse and Paul's discussion of the rapture in 1 Thessalonians 5. With these timely words, Jesus tells us not to fear the ultimate wrath of God, but he also gently reminds us of the necessity of keeping ourselves pure as we await his imminent return.

Conclusion

Of all the eschatological topics none is more polarizing

than the subject of the rapture. This is quite ironic if not tragic, judging by the fact that there are really very few scriptural passages to go on in determining the timing of this event. In fact, both Jesus and Paul are emphatic in stating that we cannot know when the Lord will appear to deliver us. And yet we persist and insist on being able to break the unbreakable code. What is more we tend to come away so confident in our position that we are willing to chastise those who don't agree with us. God have mercy!

In my exegesis of the central passage relating to the rapture, 1 Thessalonians 4-5, I have noted the obvious parallels with Christ's Olivet Discourse on the end times. So while some would like to accentuate certain differences between the rapture and the second coming, it seems clear to me that the striking similarities are much more compelling. In both the Lord suddenly appears in the clouds with a loud trumpet blast accompanied by the angels and he gathers up all believers, dead or alive, to join him in the heavens. In both instances Christ's appearing is described in the context of the 'Day of the Lord,' in which he arrives as a 'thief in the night' ready to commence the judgment of his enemies. Finally both are described as taking place suddenly and catching everyone by surprise.

The traditional pre-tribulation arguments that believers must be raptured before God's wrath is poured out and that Christ's appearing must be completely unexpected remain intact when we understand the greater context of his return. The argument from silence, that the church does not appear in the Revelation, however, does not stand muster as the final book of the New Testament is replete with references to Jewish and Gentile believers in the tribulation. What is more the Revelation seems to specifically mention the rapture placing it towards the end of the great tribulation.

So what are we to do with the notion of the rapture? Should we forget pre, mid or post-tribulation arguments and just opt for pan-tribulationalism, namely, it will all 'pan' out? I think the Biblical and logical way would be to put the rapture back into its context. It was never supposed to be the 'main event.' The exact timing of when God's people are delivered is quite insignificant when compared to God's greater purposes coming to fruition in the second coming of Christ. If we are indeed raptured earlier rather than later in the tribulation, we will thank God, but we should also be ready for the worst. Finally, based on both Christ's and Paul's words, it is clear that the Lord's appearing and our ultimate deliverance will be surprise. Let's not spoil it.

What is most helpful here, I believe, is to understand that the return of Christ is not just one event, but rather a chain of events that will be set into motion by Christ's appearing in the clouds. These included the following events in more or less this order:

- After a relatively peaceful first half of the tribulation, after the desecration of the temple, Jewish and Gentile believers will face increased persecution.
- Soon all kinds of cataclysmic events will begin to rock the planet even as the antichrist seeks to destroy God's people.
- The Sign of the Son of Man will suddenly appear in the heavens for all the world to see.
- The bodies of all believers will be instantaneously resurrected, transformed and reunited with their owners in the clouds.
- Believers alive at that time will likewise be snatched up to join Christ and his followers in the clouds.
- The Lord will shout, calling his people the Jews in particular to repentance.
- The voice of the archangel Michael will be heard proclaiming the demise of Satan's kingdom.
- The trumpet of the Lord will sound signaling the final judgments.
- The nations will quake in fear at the visible appearing of Christ as he receives the kingdom.

- The nation of Israel will mourn for Jesus and finally repent paving the way for Christ's physical return to earth.

The above synthesis of the details provide a more wholistic picture of the 'parousia'. However it must be noted that this is really only the first phase of Christ's return. Once the saints are gathered in the clouds, the judgment seat of Christ and marriage supper of the Lamb will ensue. At the same time the antichrist and his armies will be ravaging Jerusalem. Finally when all Israel truly repents, Christ and his heavenly entourage will commence their descent to the earth. As noted earlier, this will likely begin in the wilderness as Jesus delivers the Jewish people in exile and takes on their enemies. Then he will make his way to the Mount of Olives east of Jerusalem where his feet will finally touch down.

Where in Scripture is this?

When we understand the 'rapture' as part of this bigger picture we can clearly see how it fits into the larger prophetic puzzle. We can also see that his appearing may in fact be days or weeks if not months before Christ's actual descent to earth. In this case it can truly be said that the day or hour of his appearing is not known and cannot be known. It will surely be a glorious and very timely surprise for embattled believers on earth. This 'phased-return' view, I believe, is the best rendering of the facts presented by the Scriptures with regard to the timing of the rapture vis a vis the second coming.

The Parousia

C[ion] [assumption] [Another assumption]

Mike Golay tells more historic detail.

Incidentally, the overwhelming view of the early church fathers underscores their belief that believers would endure most if not all of the tribulation before being delivered in by Christ's second coming.[39] In contrast to this the notion of a pre-tribulation rapture is a fairly recent teaching proposed by John Nelson Darby in the late 19th century.[40] The traditional post-tribulation rapture position on the other hand, although enjoying historic support, has usually lacked nuanced explanatory power.

One final word of warning. In 2 Thessalonians, Paul speaks of the events that will precede the coming of Christ. He highlights two major ones: The coming of the antichrist and the great apostasy. This second development, a mass defection from the faith, is what I find especially troubling. Paul elaborates on this spiritual debacle elsewhere in his letters (1 Timothy 4:1-3). I find this particularly disturbing because it presumes that people will have a crisis of faith, namely, that their spiritual expectations will not have been met. This makes me wonder if a false hope in a pre-tribulation rapture might not *inadvertently* play into such a scenario. If believers the world over, who have been taught to believe that they will be exempted from the tribulation, suddenly find themselves in the throes of apocalyptic chaos, this might in fact send many into a spiritual tail-spin. This is why it is imperative that we not give people any false hope in this regard but rather urge them to prepare for the worst even as we hope for the best.

7. THE REVELATION

Recent events in the Middle East have highlighted once more the impotence of even the greatest and most technologically advanced nations to bring peace and prosperity to this region long ravaged by ethnic and religious rivalries. The country of Afghanistan in particular has proven once again stubbornly resistant to all attempts to democratize its people reminding us of its well earned title, 'the graveyard of empires.' Indeed the growing waves of chaos sweeping our globe remind us that we ultimately have no answer to the problem of human depravity. We urgently need for Jesus Christ to show up and set things straight.

The last book of the Bible, the Revelation, answers this desperate call and spells out in amazing details the final years of human history and God's judgments, which will give way to Christ's kingdom and ultimately our eternal home, the New Jerusalem. Ever since being penned almost two millennia ago, it has defied clear exegesis and like Afghanistan proven to be the 'graveyard' of Biblical exegetes. An obvious reason for this is that we can only expect its message to come into focus as we near the end. Indeed, we should not be surprised that the closer we come to the final showdown, the Revelation will come alive like never before.

The Revelation is not placed at the end of the whole Bible by chance. Its unique position reminds us that it is not comprehensible until we have read and understood the rest of the story. The Revelation makes more allusions and direct quotations from the Old Testament than any other New Testament book. It assumes that we have put most of the pieces of the puzzle into place so that we can see how the final pieces fit in. Thus by design it defies the haphazard interpretation of the merely curious believer or critical skeptic. Like a long physics equation, it presumes you have done your math right from the beginning and will only reward you with the answer if you have been a good student and steward of God's truths.

Another reason people struggle to decipher the Revelation is because of its unique 'apocalyptic' style. This name is taken from the book's Greek name 'apocalupsis' which means 'unveiling, revealing or disclosure.' The 'apocalyptic' genre of Biblical literature has been used to describe the writings of the prophets Daniel and Zechariah, as well as many other non-canonical first century works, which are often characterized by symbolic visions and dreams.[41] This has led some Bible students, known as Preterists, to reinterpret these 'prophetic' books in relation to their historical contexts alone with little or no bearing on the future. Thus, when they come across visions and dreams in these books, they take it upon themselves to determine how they might have been coded references to current events in the times of the authors. As can be surmised, this form of interpretation quickly degenerates into a guessing game which ultimately does little justice to the very detailed descriptions depicted in prophetic literature.

All along I have stressed the necessity of interpreting the Scriptures in a straight-forward, *literal* manner. A word on what I mean by 'literal' is in order here. Critics of this hermeneutical approach like to point out the ridiculous interpretations that can be reached in a hyper-literal analysis of symbols appearing in the prophetic books. Are we really to expect a seven headed beast to appear in Times Square? Of course not. Clearly those of us who interpret the Bible literally understand the role that symbols and metaphors play in all literature. Just as we use figures of speech in our daily life and understand them for what they are, we likewise seek to interpret the symbolic elements in

Scripture in their historical context and in accordance with the author's stated intent. Any other approach is an affront to God's Word and ultimately makes us the judge and jury of Biblical interpretation. In short, since critics are quick to make light of the word 'literal' maybe it is best to stress that we are seeking the 'plain and common sense' interpretation of Scriptures.

Going back to the title of the Revelation, we must ask what it is revealing or unveiling? First and foremost this book is the 'unveiling' of Jesus Christ. In other words, we are welcomed into the chambers of heaven to see our Savior in his present glorified state. This was important for John and the early church as they had been waiting for over half a century for Christ to return and may have begun to have their doubts. Thus from beginning to end Jesus is the center-piece of this book. In fact this is the only book of the New Testament that is directly dictated by Jesus to his apostle John. Christ's message is ever clear: I am in control and I will be victorious!

But there is more to the Revelation; Jesus specifies its purpose in the first verse as follows: *"The revelation of Jesus Christ, which God gave him to show to his servants the things that must soon take place."* Clearly, the Revelation was designed to give us essential information of events yet future. These are also described as happening 'soon' namely that the fulfillment of these prophetic events is always 'at hand' or imminent.[42] This is because the Scriptures always instruct us to be waiting and watching for the culmination of God's purposes (Matthew 24:50; Luke 12:40).

Whenever I teach the book of Revelation at our yearly discipleship school, I feel like a tour-guide. Having lived in Middle East for over twenty years, I often have the privilege of taking visitors to Biblical sites. One of the perks of being a guide is that I get to learn more and more about these locations and their history as I chance upon new things along the way. In a similar way, every time I take a group of students through the Revelation I discover new things and find that I see the picture ever clearer. Now for those that are new to this journey, it may seem daunting at first, but believe me you will soon be trembling with excitement. Trust me the trip is not as hard as it is often made out to be. My hope here is to guide you through the eschatological landscape of the Revelation trusting we will gain a new appreciation of the wonders that await us all. I further aim to do this in a way that is fair and faithful to the original intent of Christ the author of the Revelation.

The Outline

As noted above, the Revelation has proven ever challenging to exegetes down through the centuries. However, the Bible also intimates that as we approach the end times we will be granted the necessary insight into God's prophetic word in order to be adequately prepared. Notice the final words of the angel Gabriel to Daniel, *"Go your way, Daniel, for the words are shut up and sealed until the time of the end. Many shall purify themselves and make themselves white and be refined, but the wicked shall act wickedly. And none of the wicked shall understand, **but those who are wise shall understand**"* (Daniel 12:9-10).

In order to make sense of the Revelation we do well to let it speak for itself. At the very outset of the book, the Lord Jesus makes it clear that he will be giving us prophetic information about 'the things that must soon take place.' This is an important interpretive clue pointing to Revelation 1:19 which lays out quite elegantly the outline of the book: *"Write therefore the things that you have seen, those that are and those that are to take place after this."* We can readily observe three consecutive subject matters that Jesus commands John to elaborate upon: 1. The things you have seen, 2. The things that are, and 3. The things that are to take place after these this. A quick look at the book will show that chapter one relates to the 'things John had seen.' Chapters 2-3, the letters to the churches under John's care in Asia Minor constitute 'the things that are.' Then starting with chapter 4 through the end, the Revelation transports us to 'the things that will take place afterwards,' namely yet future events.

The first section of this outline is focused intently on revealing the person of Christ in all his resurrected glory. This is because, more important than knowing all the details of the future, we need to be sure that we know the one who holds the future quite literally in the palm of his hand:

> Thus says the LORD: "Let not the wise man boast in his wisdom, let not the mighty man boast in his might, let not the rich man boast in his riches, but let him who boasts boast in this, that he understands and knows me, that I am the LORD who practices steadfast love, justice, and righteousness in the earth. For in these things I delight, declares the LORD" (Jeremiah 9:23-24).

The first chapter of Revelation makes a point of establishing the 'main event' of the end times as follows, "Behold, he is coming with the clouds, and every eye will see him, even those who pierced him, and all tribes of the earth will wail on account of him. Even so. Amen" (1:7). Then we are privy to John's vision in which, despite having been one of the closest disciples of Jesus, when confronted with the heavenly splendor of Christ, he falls at his feet like a dead man! He clearly recognizes Jesus, but to see him majestically arrayed as a Royal Priest just overwhelms him.

At the outset of the Revelation there is an instructive point with reference to the 'apocalyptic' description of Jesus. Christ is seen holding seven stars and walking among seven lampstands. Many modern interpreters might be quick to get creative here in their interpretations of what these symbols might mean. However, if we exercise patience and read to the end of the chapter, we are told exactly what they mean, "As for the mystery of the seven stars that you saw in my right hand, and the seven golden lampstands, the seven stars are the angels of the seven churches, and the seven lampstands are the seven churches" (Revelation 1:20).

The point that is being made is that every symbol has an

intended meaning and object. In other words, when we come across these type of symbolic representations, this does not suddenly give us the prerogative to begin interpreting them ad hoc according to our own exegetical fancies. Instead we are to follow the Biblical clues and allow the text to point us to the intended meaning. A similar illustration of this important point is seen later in the description of the great harlot Babylon in Revelation 17. Any number of books and articles representing different and often divergent theories as to her identity have been produced. Some claim she represents capitalism and others communism, some claim she stands for the Catholic Church, others that she embodies Islam. However, what is often missed by many is that at the end of the chapter we are told that she represents a city. Whatever else the harlot might symbolize clearly Babylon is first and foremost linked to the city of the antichrist.

Returning to the outline, while the first section relates to John's vision of Jesus, the second section refers to the status of the churches in the first century. The Lord Jesus has chosen to address this book to seven churches in Asian Minor, on the Aegean coast of modern Turkey. Prior to being exiled to the island of Patmos where he received this revelation, John had been living in Ephesus and likely ministering to this group of churches regularly. Thus he was intimately aware of their condition and keenly interested in what the Lord had to say to them. Of course, the words of Jesus, although primarily targeting these seven churches in the first century, are ultimately applicable to all the churches who have an ear to hear what the Spirit is saying.

The third section of the outline, beginning in chapter 4, starts with the words 'after these things,' which clearly links it to the final and futuristic section. John is suddenly transported into the heavenly throne room of God and is soon struggling to find words to describe the glories of God's presence. There he is caught up in the universal chorus of praise as all creation extols the King of Heaven. Interestingly here he also witnesses a group of twenty four elders as they bow before the heavenly throne. This unique group seem to embody the union of Israel (12 Tribes) and the Church (12 Apostles) as they gather together in adoration of God. In chapter five however, a sealed scroll in the right hand of God is brought to his attention, which for some reason causes John great consternation. What does it contain? Whatever it is, it is clearly very important and significant to the development of the Revelation.[43]

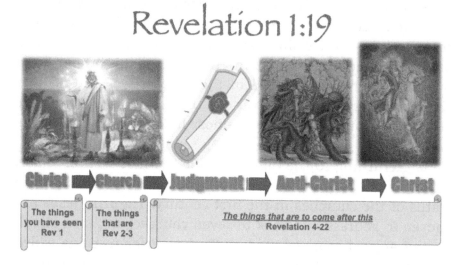

The Sealed Scroll

Once again many have attempted to decipher the meaning of the seven-sealed scroll but this has often only led to more confusion. First we note the details of its description; it is written inside and out and sealed with seven seals. The scroll is clearly brimming with highly classified information. Throughout the Revelation, we will often come across the number seven; seven stars, seven seals, seven trumpets, seven angels, and more, all highlighting the 'completed' or 'consummating' nature of the Revelation. The seven seals of the scroll speak to the extreme significance of its guarded contents as well as the 'finalized' nature of its decree.

In the following verses it becomes clear that no one is worthy to break the seals and open the scroll. When no one in heaven or on earth is deemed worthy to bring to light the contents of the scroll John suddenly breaks out in great weeping. What elicits such a reaction? As the whole universe seemingly holds its breath, Jesus suddenly appears and is alone deemed worthy to reveal the contents of this all important scroll. The heavenly hosts erupt in glorious celebration and Christ is extolled for his immortal sacrifice. But again we are left wondering what the scroll actually represents.

Many suggestions have been made as to the meaning of this scroll. Some suggest it is a divine will, sealed seven times over like an ancient Roman will or final testament. Others have suggested the scroll represents the title deed of the universe, which is ultimately entrusted to the rightful ruler, Jesus Christ. While these interpretations may seem attractive, as stressed earlier, we need to let the Biblical text be our guide. In other words, when the scroll is finally opened in the next chapters what are its contents? Put succinctly, the subject matter of the scroll is God's judgment to be meted out on mankind.[44] The scroll represents God's final indictment of humanity.

This explains why John was so distraught at the thought that no one would be deemed worthy to execute God's justice on the earth. However in the end, when Jesus arrives, John is elated to know that the record will be set straight. Interestingly the designation of Jesus as the 'executer' of God's judgment was referenced in the gospel of John. Note the following verses: *"For the Father judges no one, but has given all judgment to the Son, that all may honor the Son, just as they honor the Father"* (John 5:22-23a). *"For as the Father has life in himself, so he has granted the Son also to have life in himself. And he has given him authority to execute judgment, because he is the Son of Man"* (John 5:26-27a).

Some may question the right of Jesus to judge mankind, however Revelation 5 implies that he alone is qualified to do so on the grounds that he is not only fully God and fully man, but also because he alone offered himself for all mankind. Thus, the very fact that he was slain for mankind's sins and that he purchased for God people from every tribe and nation qualifies him uniquely to then be able to judge those who have rejected his gracious offer of salvation.

So the scroll represents the accumulation of God's judgments on mankind now entrusted to Jesus for him to execute upon the earth. Thus with each consecutive seal that he opens he reveals God's plan for the final judgment of mankind. This starts with false promises of peace which soon turn to war, famine and utter ruin. Believers are also caught up in this conflagration and many are martyred even as the whole earth is finally plunged into utter darkness and devastation of apocalyptic proportions.

A word on the chronology of the Revelation is in order here. Many attempts have been made to outline and organize the material of the Revelation, however, as always I believe it is best to assume a chronological progression unless otherwise noted by the text. I would liken this to taking a road trip down some historic highway. The point of origin and destination are set beforehand. However, as you hit the road you will be confronted with a variety of 'alternate' or 'scenic' routes. Taking any one of these detours will not alter your destination but will serve to enrich your appreciation of the land. There will also be signs to 'scenic viewpoints' or other historical markers which are well worth visiting. This will help you gain a greater understanding of the region you are traversing.

In a similar way, the point of origin and the point of destination of the Revelation are quite clear; we are traveling through the seven year period of tribulation to the return of Christ and ultimately to his kingdom. However, as the narrative develops, there will be times when the trip will be interrupted for a short 'panoramic experience' or 'historical purview.' Once necessary explanations are made, the trajectory will continue moving forward. As we continue our study of the Revelation these will be noted in due course.

Regarding the seven seals it is best to see them as laying out a road-map for the seven year tribulation. Whenever you start a trip you surely need a map. Chapter 6 takes us from the beginning of the tribulation all the way to the end. It is history written in advance. This is borne out by the fact that the cataclysmic events described in the 6th Seal clearly relate to the final judgments reiterated later in the book (11:19, 16:17-21). These are subsequently seen embedded in the 7th Seal and take place in turn starting with the seven trumpets and concluding with the seven bowls. Thus, the 7th Seal will later divulge the details of the final year or months of the tribulation.

Going back to the first four seals, most are familiar with the four horsemen of the apocalypse. It is important to note that from the heavenly vantage point from which John writes, these are being let loose upon the command of Jesus. It is Christ who sets in motion and ultimately guides this final sequence of events, not Satan. The white horse and his rider seem to promise peace and prosperity as they conquer many nations. This is likely a veiled reference to the coming antichrist who's covenant with the nations, as described in Daniel 9:27, will initiate the final week of Daniel's prophetic timetable. However his plans for global peace will soon turn sour even as the red horse of war shows up. Things will only get worse as war will give way to horrible plagues and famine so that death will stalk mankind. In short, the four horsemen describe the general trajectory of the seven years of the tribulation. This will result in two things: great suffering for the saints and God's judgments raining down on mankind.

As noted earlier the utter destruction caused by the cataclysmic events of the 6th Seal make it clear that it has brought us to the cusp of Christ's triumphal return and the end of the tribulation. This is the time of 'the wrath of the Lamb' and the question is raised, 'Who is able to stand?' This causes the chronology of the narrative to pause, as chapter 7 takes us on a short detour highlighting the believers who against all odds will be able to stand for Christ in this most trying time of human history. These will include 144,000 Jewish believers whose ministry will result in a global harvest of souls from all tongues and nations. It will be the ultimate version of Pentecost as Joel's predictions quoted earlier by Peter in Acts 2 are finally realized in their fullness. Indeed in the darkest hour of human history the light of the gospel will shine the brightest.

The Trumpets Blow

In chapter 8, the narrative now picks up where we left off and continues with a detailed chronology of God's final judgments as revealed in the 7th Seal. These events come in response to the blowing of trumpets as follows:

1. *The first angel blew his trumpet, and there followed hail and fire, mixed with blood, and these were thrown upon the earth. And a third of the earth was burned up, and a third of the trees were burned up, and all green grass was burned up.*

2. *The second angel blew his trumpet, and something like a great mountain, burning with fire, was thrown into the sea, and a third of the sea became blood. A third of the living creatures in the sea died, and a third of the ships were destroyed.*

3. *The third angel blew his trumpet, and a great star fell from heaven, blazing like a torch, and it fell on a third of the rivers and on the springs of water. The name of the star is Wormwood. A third of the waters became wormwood, and many people died from the water, because it had been made bitter.*

4. *The fourth angel blew his trumpet, and a third of the sun was struck, and a third of the moon, and a third of the stars, so that a third of their light might be darkened, and a third of the day might be kept from shining, and likewise a third of the night* (Revelation

8:7-12).

The destructive magnitude of these judgments cannot be overstated. Heaven and earth, the seas and the rivers will all be dramatically affected. We can see at this stage that God's judgment is only partial, affecting 1/3 of its target. Later in the outpouring of the final bowl judgments, however, we will see that the devastation will be total and complete. The narrative continues:

> *Then I looked, and I heard an eagle crying with a loud voice as it flew directly overhead, "Woe, woe, woe to those who dwell on the earth, at the blasts of the other trumpets that the three angels are about to blow!"* (Revelation 8:13).

The angel warns that the next three trumpet blasts will be even worse. He describes them as three 'Woes!' These are laid out in detail in the following chapter as follows:

5. First Woe - The first half of chapter 9 seems to describe a horror movie, only it is for real. The bottomless pit is opened up releasing untold numbers of demonic spirits in possession of mutated locust-like lethal creatures. These in turn begin to swarm across the earth and inflict horrendous pain on its inhabitants. Whether this is a symbolic description of the 'northern army' of the antichrist alluded to in Joel 2:1-25, or an actual mutant army of genetically altered creatures possessed by demons, or a combination of both, is yet to be seen. Either way John's incredibly detailed description would lead us to expect a literal fulfillment with terrifying ramifications.

6. Second Woe - The second half of the chapter describes a second global onslaught at the hands of mutated creatures. The fact that they are led by four previously bound evil spirits and ultimately kill a

third of all mankind is enough to give pause. Their ranks are further described as a formidable force of two hundred million horsemen. Whether this will be some army from the far east or a demonic mutant force, or again a combination of both, is yet to be seen. We learn more about them later in the 6th Bowl.

7. Third Woe - The third the final woe is the also the last trumpet. This does not sound until later in chapter 11 as it highlights the culmination of God's judgments, namely the pouring out of God's wrath, as represented by the 7 bowls. This will be the beginning of the end.

Before proceeding to the last judgments which will bring God's purposes to completion, the Revelation narrative takes a short breather to take stock of how far we have come. By now we are already nearing the end of the tribulation and a series of very important events are all ready to take place in quick succession. However the contexts and characters involved in these events need to be explored in order to fully appreciate the narrative, thus the chronology remains on hold for a bit.

In chapter 10 we hear what is likely the voice of the archangel Michael as he declares that God's purposes are about to reach their climax. He has a small scroll in his hand which is likely what is left of the seven sealed indictment opened previously by Jesus Christ. He urges a beleaguered John to swallow it, just as the ancient prophet Ezekiel had done, and to keep prophesying (Ezekiel 3:1-3).

In Chapter 11, the apostle John is given a measuring rod much like Ezekiel and is told to measure the temple. This seems to be a reference to the temple that will be built during the tribulation period but will ultimately be desecrated and destroyed by the antichrist. Thus it is described as being trodden underfoot by the nations for 42 months, that is, the final three and a half years of the tribulation. The majority of the Jews will have likely fled Jerusalem after the mid-point debacle at the temple. In their stead we find two men of God, dressed in sackcloth of mourning for the desecrated temple, standing tall in Jerusalem challenging the antichrist.

Much has been written about whether these men are Enoch, Elijah or Moses or someone else. Personally I doubt they are resurrected saints based on the fact that in the first instance of the promised Elijah, fulfilled by the coming of John the Baptist, it resulted not in a resurrected Elijah but in another person functioning in the spirit and power of Elijah (Luke 1:17). Thus, I expect these last day prophets to be two unique Jewish men whose ministry is reminiscent of Elijah/John's ministry which was only partially fulfilled in the first coming of Christ. Only this time instead of one Elijah it will truly be a double portion of him.

From Revelation 11 we further learn that their last stand in the temple of Jerusalem finally comes to an end at the conclusion of the tribulation when they are killed and their corpses left in the city square for all to see and celebrate their demise. But these last day prophets will have the last laugh as they are miraculously resurrected for all the whole world see even as Jerusalem is left in the throes of a deadly earthquake.

At this time the final trumpet is sounded and Christ is officially declared King of the World: *"The kingdom of the world has become the kingdom of our Lord and of his Christ, and he shall reign forever and ever"* (Revelation 11:15). This will initiate the first stage of his return, namely his appearing in the clouds, otherwise known as the 'sign of the Son of Man' (Matthew 24:30). Christ appears as the victorious warrior ready to do battle for his suffering people. At this time the original temple in heaven will be made visible for all to witness as Christ is enthroned as the Royal Priest of his people.[45] The ark of the covenant, long missing from God's temples on earth, will also be unveiled in his presence, in order to pave the way for the New Covenant to be ratified with his people Israel when they finally repent and welcome him home. This is further a reminder that the way into God's presence has indeed been opened for all who trust in Christ (Hebrews 9:11-14).

A word is in order here on why Christ is always portrayed as appearing in the clouds of heaven (Matthew 24:30, 26:64; Revelation 1:7, 14:14). This is not because his second coming is slated for an overcast day. Rather the repeated references to the cloud seem to be a clear allusion to the cloud of glory that symbolized God's presence in the Old Testament. There are many allusions made to God appearing in a fiery cloud to Abraham (Genesis 15:17), then to Moses and the people of Israel (Exodus 3:2, 13:21-22, 24:16-18), but especially in relation to the tabernacle and temple (Exodus 40:34-38; 1 Kings 8:10-11). In the New Testament it is noteworthy that Jesus is taken up to heaven in the clouds and expected to return in like manner (Acts 1:9). The mention of the cloud in relation to Christ's coming is a direct link to the glory of God which was seen by all the people in the temple. Thus we are not surprised to read that as the Son of Man appears the heavenly sanctuary is likewise opened and Christ is seen coming in the clouds of heaven. In other words, Jesus is seen as the embodiment of God's glory coming in the ancient clouds of fire to protect his people and judge their enemies.

The Beauty And The Beast

The Revelation narrative has now brought us all the way to final phase of the tribulation but there are still some important characters that need to be introduced to appreciate the resolution of the story. In chapter 11, John made mention of the 'beast' who attacked the two witnesses. Now he will take some time to elaborate its background. In order to do this he needs to start back even further with the 'dragon' or Satan who is the real power house behind the antichrist. Thus, in chapter 12, we are privy to a brief panoramic retelling of the Biblical version of the 'beauty and the beast.'

And a great sign appeared in heaven: a woman clothed with the sun, with the moon under her feet, and on her head a crown of twelve stars. She was pregnant and was crying out in birth pains and the agony of giving birth. And another sign appeared in heaven: behold, a great red dragon, with seven heads and ten horns, and on his heads seven diadems. His tail swept down a third of the stars of heaven and cast them to the earth. And the dragon stood before the woman who was about to give birth, so that when she bore her child he might devour it. She gave birth to a male child, one who is to rule all the nations with a rod of iron, but her child was caught up to God and to his throne, and the woman fled into the wilderness, where she has a place prepared by God, in which she is to be nourished for 1,260 days (Revelation 12:1-6).

Most commentators are quick to pick up on the identification of the woman as representing Israel. She is large with child, the Messiah, who is destined to rule all nations. The great red dragon on the other hand clearly represents the devil who's goal from the beginning has been to usurp man's right to rule. His multiple heads and crowns highlight the fact that he is the one ultimately behind the many empires that have sought to rule the planet. He is particularly intent on destroying his arch rival, Jesus Christ, the seed of the woman, however, the child eludes his grasp and is taken up to God's presence. In the meantime Israel, represented by the woman, is forced to flee to the wilderness where she is sheltered by God for 1,260 days. This now brings us back to the final phase of the tribulation. But there is more:

Now war arose in heaven, Michael and his angels fighting against the dragon. And the dragon and his angels fought back, but he was defeated, and there was no longer any place for them in heaven. And the great dragon was thrown down, that ancient serpent, who is called the devil and Satan, the deceiver of the whole world—he was thrown down to the earth, and his angels were thrown down with him. And I heard a loud voice in heaven, saying, "Now the salvation and the power and the kingdom of our God and the authority of his Christ have come, for the accuser of our brothers has been thrown down, who accuses them day and night before our God (Revelation 12:7-10).

This passage pulls back the cosmic curtain allowing us a sneak preview of the spiritual war taking place in the heavens during the tribulation. The archangel Michael, the great defender of Israel, is seen fighting against the devil and his demonic hordes. As we noted earlier in relation to the 'restrainer' of 2 Thessalonians 2:6, it is likely that Michael who was restraining Satan's efforts prior to the tribulation had been ordered to 'stand down.' Now however, when Christ suddenly appears in the clouds, the archangel gives the command to the heavenly hosts to rout Satan who then looses his foothold of power in the heavens and is thrust down to earth. This of course spells trouble for God's people on earth as the devil knows his time is short and will pour out all his wrath on believers at that time. But the drama regarding the woman continues,

And when the dragon saw that he had been thrown down to the earth, he pursued the woman who had given birth to the male child. But the woman was given the two wings of the great eagle so that she might fly from the serpent into the wilderness, to the place where she is to be nourished for a time, and times, and half a time. The serpent poured water like a river out of his mouth after the woman, to sweep her away with a flood. But the earth came to the help of the woman, and the earth opened its mouth and swallowed the river that the dragon had poured from his mouth. Then the dragon became furious with the woman and went off to make war on the rest of her offspring, on those who keep the commandments of God and hold to the testimony of Jesus (Revelation 12:13-17).

The final years and months of the tribulation are

epitomized by the devil's persistent efforts to destroy Israel. This is because he knows that if Israel can be annihilated then God's promises will fall to the ground. At this time however, the Lord is supernaturally aiding his people, carrying them on eagle's wings, much like he did after the exodus in the wilderness (Exodus 19:4). Thus Israel is given divine protection during her time of exile in the wilderness for the remaining three and a half years of the tribulation. Finally, Satan realizes the futility of his attacks and turns his fury on 'the rest of her offspring', namely the church of Christ.

In chapter 13, John is finally introduced to the 'beast from the sea', the earthly perpetrator of Israel's persecution alluded to in Revelation 11:7. This is none other than the antichrist of whom we have already spoken in great detail earlier. In summary, he establishes himself at the head of a great coalition of ten nations promising peace in the Middle East. In time, however, his true blasphemous nature is revealed even as he desecrates the temple in Jerusalem and begins to persecute the saints. His reign is further bolstered by the appearing of a second beast who works wonders also referred to as 'the false prophet.' Together they set up a regime in which people are forced either to worship the first beast or suffer the dire consequences.

Much has been made of the 666 mark of the beast which will be enforced at this time. Some have gone so far as to suggest that Covid vaccines or micro-chips are the mark of the beast.[46] First it must be noted that this mark is knowingly taken by people who worship the beast (Revelation 14:9-10, 20:4). So there is no need to worry that we might accidentally take it. Secondly, the command to 'calculate' the number which corresponds to the name of the beast points us to the ancient practice known as gematria.[47] This is clearly a clue given to believers who will endure the rigors of the tribulation so that they will be able to verify the identity of the beast. However we must note that until we know the name of the beast it will be impossible to decipher or 'calculate' the numerical value of his name. Consequently, in the mean time, there is no use getting caught up in guesswork or conspiracy theories.

Chapter 14 brings us back to the final phase of the tribulation. Even as the antichrist's loyalists are being branded with his name, John notes that Christ's followers, the 144,000 in particular, bear the name of his Father on their foreheads. Presumably martyred, they are here seen gathered around the Lord Jesus in Mt. Zion, likely a spiritual description of Christ's kingdom outpost in the clouds as he prepares to descend to earth. At this time the 'shout of God' or 'cry of command' rings out even as the eternal gospel is proclaimed one last time. Israel in particular is called to recognize the one they have pierced and welcome him back. Likewise suffering saints are warned again not to fall in league with the antichrist but to persevere to the end. At this time all believers are suddenly 'reaped', the dead are raised even as living believers are raptured and all gathered together to Christ's presence in the clouds (1 Thessalonians 4:16-17). *different setting here.*

Armageddon

Exactly when in the tribulation period Christ will actually appear is not specified because by design it must be a surprise. However, it is evident that he will come towards the end as he prepares to enter the fray. Indeed the final months of the tribulation will be consumed with God's judgment pouring down from heaven even as the antichrist and his armies seek to obliterate those who are left of ethnic Israel and the church. Once Christ appears in the clouds it will be a war between heaven and earth with Jesus commanding his forces from the heavens even as the unholy trinity of beasts wreak havoc on earth. Such will be the stage of the final war known as armageddon.

In chapter 15 we are invited to see the battle from heaven's vantage point as angels prepare great bowls of wrath to pour out on the earth. As noted earlier God's temple is already visible in the clouds at this time and so are the angels bearing great vials of judgment. These are the final and most devastating plagues of all time.

1. *The first angel went and poured out his bowl on the earth, and harmful and painful sores came upon the people who bore the mark of the beast and worshiped its image.*
2. *The second angel poured out his bowl into the sea, and it became like the blood of a corpse, and every living thing died that was in the sea.*
3. *The third angel poured out his bowl into the rivers and the springs of water, and they became blood.*
4. *The fourth angel poured out his bowl on the sun, and it was allowed to scorch people with fire. They were scorched by the fierce heat, and they cursed the name of God who had power over these plagues. They did not repent and give him glory.*
5. *The fifth angel poured out his bowl on the throne of the beast, and its kingdom was plunged into darkness. People gnawed their tongues in anguish and cursed the God of heaven for their pain and sores. They did not repent of their deeds.*
6. *The sixth angel poured out his bowl on the great river Euphrates, and its water was dried up, to prepare the way for the kings from the east* (Revelation 16:2-12).

It is important to note that these final judgments, much like the final plagues in Egypt, particularly target the enemy's regime. They are also no longer partial but complete in their scope of destruction. The plagues of Egypt however, pale in comparison with the global devastation predicted for this last phase of the great tribulation. And yet, instead of repenting and seeking God's mercy, the inhabitants of earth raise their fist to heaven in perpetual defiance.

The 6th Bowl evidently paves the way for the armies of

the east. These may have been alluded to in the 6th Trumpet where a horde of mutated demonic armies numbering 200 million were seen ravaging the planet. Now they bring their wrath to bear on Israel. John learns more about how this final battle will come to pass,

> *And I saw, coming out of the mouth of the dragon and out of the mouth of the beast and out of the mouth of the false prophet, three unclean spirits like frogs. For they are demonic spirits, performing signs, who go abroad to the kings of the whole world, to assemble them for battle on the great day of God the Almighty. And they assembled them at the place that in Hebrew is called Armageddon* (Revelation 16:13-14, 16).

First we note that the real forces behind this final military conflagration are demonic. They gather armies from around the world to Israel in a last ditch effort to upend God's eternal plans. However, what they don't know is that this is actually the 'Great Day of the Lord' in which God is actually gathering them together in one place to obliterate them all at once (Joel 3:1-17; Ezekiel 38). The prophet Zechariah gives elaborate details of this final military campaign against Israel pointing out that along with the siege of Jerusalem there will be war all across the land of Judea (Zechariah 12). More importantly this final war will serve to bring Israel to full repentance as they see Jesus in the clouds and mourn for him, begging him to return to save them.

In the Revelation John notes that the armies of the antichrist are assembled in the place known in his native Hebrew tongue as 'har magedon.' This Greek transliteration has proved notoriously difficult to decipher. Over the past century it has been popular to identify it with the great valley of Jezreel in the north of Israel, largely because it lies below the ancient town of Megiddo at the foot of Mt. Carmel. This linkage however is problematic, largely because the word 'har' in Hebrew means mountain and Megiddo is not a mountain but rather an ancient city at the head of a valley. It could be a reference to the mountain standing above Megiddo, namely Mt. Carmel, where God won many a victory over his pagan enemies in the past. Others suggest Mt. Tabor, another prominent mountain on the northern edge of the valley of Jezreel. One suggestion is to see armageddon as a transliteration of the Hebrew 'har moged' which means 'the mount of assembly.' This would point to Mt. Zion, namely Jerusalem.[48]

In the end, the exact location will matter little as it is clear that the final campaign of armageddon will overwhelm Israel and finally key in on Jerusalem. However, it is important to recognize that it will indeed be a prolonged military campaign lasting weeks if not months. As the antichrist positions the arriving armies around Israel and besieges Jerusalem, the Lord Jesus will be making his way across the wilderness where he engages the first of his enemies at Bozrah, east of Israel in the modern nation of Jordan, as described by the prophet Isaiah.

> *Who is this who comes from Edom, in crimsoned garments from Bozrah, he who is splendid in his apparel, marching in the greatness of his strength? "It is I, speaking in righteousness, mighty to save." Why is your apparel red, and your garments like his who treads in the winepress? "I have trodden the winepress alone, and from the peoples no one was with me; I trod them in my anger and trampled them in my wrath; their lifeblood spattered on my garments, and stained all my apparel. For the day of vengeance was in my heart, and my year of redemption had come. I looked, but there was no one to help; I was appalled, but there was no one to uphold; so my own arm brought me salvation, and my wrath upheld me. I trampled down the peoples in my anger; I made them drunk in my wrath, and I poured out their lifeblood on the earth"* (Isaiah 63:1-6).

From there Jesus will eventually proceed to the Mount of Olives where he will stand in judgment over the antichrist's armies assailing his people in Jerusalem. Again, how long all these final military maneuvers will take is difficult to determine, but what is certain is the victorious outcome of the King of Kings.

The Glorious Return

By now we have hopefully begun to see that the second coming of Christ is not just a simple descent from heaven. On the contrary it will happen in stages or phases culminating with the liberation of his people Israel and his establishment on David's throne in Jerusalem. The stages of the second coming may be laid out as follows:

1. The Appearing - This first phase is best described as a sudden revelation of Christ in the clouds. It is likely what Jesus referred to when he spoke of 'the sign of the Son of Man'. The apostle Paul calls it the 'manifestation,' or epiphany in Greek (1 Timothy 6:14; 2 Timothy 4:1,8; Titus 2:13).

2. The Gathering - Simultaneously deceased believers of all periods will be resurrected even as living believers are all gathered together to meet Jesus in the clouds (1 Thessalonians 4:16-17; 2 Thessalonians 2:1). The Revelation describes this as a great 'reaping of souls' (Revelation 14:14). It will be in the context of this great 'family reunion' in the clouds that the 'judgment seat of Christ' and the 'marriage supper of the Lamb' will take place. These forthcoming events may take weeks if not months to unfold in the heavens.

3. The Coming - Also known as the 'parousia', literally 'coming near' in Greek, it can be used in general to refer to the second advent of Christ or more specifically to this final phase which relates to Christ's physical descent to earth. At this time Christ will come down with his heavenly armies pouring

out judgment on his enemies even as he delivers his embattled people Israel (2 Thessalonians 1:5-10). This will also be a time of cataclysmic plagues (2 Peter 3:12). The 'parousia' will culminate with Christ's arrival in Jerusalem.

The notion of Christ first appearing in the heavens and gathering all believers to himself before beginning his full and final descent to earth is further evidenced by an ancient imperial custom. In ancient times when an emperor or conquering general was about to return to his capital, the leaders of the people would all go out to meet him and the usher him back into the city amid great pomp and circumstance. King David experienced this loving welcome on his return from fighting his treacherous son Absalom (2 Samuel 19). Jesus also alluded to this custom when speaking of his second coming in the parable of the nobleman (Luke 19:11-13). Similarly, before returning to earth, Christ will gather his servants in the clouds to settle accounts with them and determine how to divide the spoil of the forthcoming victory (Luke 19:17, 19).

Back to the narrative of Revelation we have come to the 7th Bowl which describes the final and most devastating of God's judgments as they pave the way for the return of Christ to Zion. John records as follows:

> The seventh angel poured out his bowl into the air, and a loud voice came out of the temple, from the throne, saying, "It is done!" And there were flashes of lightning, rumblings, peals of thunder, and a great earthquake such as there had never been since man was on the earth, so great was that earthquake. The great city was split into three parts, and the cities of the nations fell, and God remembered Babylon the great, to make her drain the cup of the wine of the fury of his wrath. And every island fled away, and no mountains were to be found. And great hailstones, about one hundred pounds each, fell from heaven on people; and they cursed God for the plague of the hail,

because the plague was so severe (Revelation 16:17-21).

This marks the end of the great tribulation. The 'great city' that is seen being torn apart by earthquakes is clearly a reference to Jerusalem. It is described as being split in three pieces a possible nod to Zechariah's prophetic words with reference to the spiritual refining of Israel in the last days (Zechariah 13:8-9). Likewise, 'Babylon the great' is also given her share of God's judgment. In the following chapter John will be given more detail about this pagan city which plays the harlot with the nations on behalf of the antichrist in the end times. In the end, her destruction, at the hands of her own leaders, elicits great consternation the world over (Revelation 18).

The final cataclysmic events will reach their climax when the islands and the mountains crumble before the glory of Christ's return. This brings us to the end of the events originally mapped out in Revelation 6. It also echoes the foreboding warnings of Peter regarding the 'Day of the Lord': *"But the day of the Lord will come like a thief, and then the heavens will pass away with a roar, and the heavenly bodies will be burned up and dissolved, and the earth and the works that are done on it will be exposed"* (2 Peter 3:10). The apostle John further speaks of one hundred pound hailstones pummeling the earth even as men continue to blaspheme God and mourn the loss of their adulterous capital Babylon.

Chapter 19 of Revelation opens with four 'Hallelujahs.' This is set in direct contrast to the great mourning regarding the destruction of Babylon in the previous chapter. This heavenly celebration takes us back to the joy of the believers gathered around Christ in the clouds previous to his final descent. They extoll God for his judgment of the antichrist and his kingdom and they also delight in the joys of the marriage of the Lamb (19:7). Once the heavenly festivities are concluded the Lord girds his sword and begins his descent to earth (See: Psalm 45).

Then I saw heaven opened, and behold, a white horse! The one sitting on it is called Faithful and True, and in righteousness he judges and makes war. His eyes are like a flame of fire, and on his head are many diadems, and he has a name written that no one knows but himself. He is clothed in a robe dipped in blood, and the name by which he is called is The Word of God. And the armies of heaven, arrayed in fine linen, white and pure, were following him on white horses. From his mouth comes a sharp sword with which to strike down the nations, and he will rule them with a rod of iron. He will tread the winepress of the fury of the wrath of God the Almighty. On his robe and on his thigh he has a name written, King of kings and Lord of lords (Revelation 19:11-16).

Unlike the first white horse of chapter 6, which turned out to be an impostor, now the true Prince of Peace emerges on his glorious steed. He comes with a mind to execute God's judgment on his enemies. He is described as the ultimate and long awaited King with many crowns. His robe is dipped in the blood of his enemies which he has already trampled in Bozrah. At this time the 'armies of heaven', namely all resurrected believers, follow in his train. He also brings with him the newly released Jewish exiles (See: Psalm 68). Thus his regal procession makes its way through the wilderness back to Jerusalem to deliver those who are left of the Jewish people in Jerusalem. The final phrase of Christ's triumphal entry and the deliverance of his embattled people are most poignantly described in the final chapters of Zechariah.

In the end there will be no need for us to fight on behalf of the Lord Jesus. His word of judgment, extending like a sword from his mouth, will literally melt the armies of the antichrist where they stand. The remaining verses of Revelation 19 hark back to Ezekiel 39 in which the birds of prey are called upon to feast on the corpses of the vanquished hordes. The antichrist and his false prophet are likewise seized and summarily condemned to eternal punishment in the fires of hell. In this way the final human empire and great tribulation will come to an end.

One last word is in order on the timing of these events especially in connection with the final words of Daniel's prophecy: "*And from the time that the regular burnt offering is taken away and the abomination that makes desolate is set up, there shall be 1,290 days. Blessed is he who waits and arrives at the 1,335 days.*" (Daniel 12:11-12). The second half of the tribulation is usually described as lasting three and a half years (12:7) More specifically the desecration of Jerusalem is said to last 42 months or 1260 days (Revelation 11:2-3). Here however Daniel adds another 30 days to this time frame which seems to be the window in which Christ's return will take place. He further adds 45 more days to allow for the final establishment of Christ's kingdom thus counting them 'blessed' who attain to that glorious new day.

The Millennium

As the dust of the great tribulation settles, Christ will emerge firmly established on the throne of his ancestor David in Jerusalem. At this time he will judge those that are left on the earth. Remember, that not everyone will join in the antichrist's attack on Israel and although the planet will have been ravaged, some will survive to see Christ receive the kingdom. At this time all of Israel, or those who are left of her, will have put their full trust in Christ and welcomed him as their Messiah (Romans 11:26). What is left of the Gentiles however, will be gathered before King Jesus for judgment. Those who have shown even the most basic kindness to persecuted saints during the tribulation will be allowed to continue living under his gracious reign, while those who did not do so will be delivered to judgment (Matthew 25:31-46).

It is important to note here that the earthly kingdom of Christ is not equivalent to heaven. The new heavens and the new earth will only come into play after the destruction of the current one at the end of the 1,000 year reign of Christ. So when Jesus becomes king on earth there will still be unbelievers left over from the tribulation and they will have a choice whether to put their personal faith in Christ or not. In fact, Daniel hints at the continuation of previous kingdoms in some subservient during this time (Daniel 7:12). Ultimately, however, they will have to submit to the laws and regulations of God's kingdom on earth or suffer the consequences.

Returning to the Revelation, quite interestingly we do not find a great deal of information regarding the millennial reign of Christ. The primary reason for this is likely the fact that the prophets in the Old Testament have already said more than enough. Indeed the prophetic books are full of descriptions of Jerusalem being elevated physically and politically to become the capital city of a global messianic kingdom. There are also many evocative descriptions of the peaceful conditions of the millennium with the lamb cuddling up to the lion and children playing with cobras (Isaiah 2, 11). In his final words, the prophet Zechariah further describes the nations gathering to Jerusalem to join God's people in celebrating the yearly feasts in honor of Yahweh.

The prophet Ezekiel also gives an incredibly detailed description of the millennial temple where all nations will gather to worship the one true God (Ezekiel 40-48). Although this final temple is clearly modeled after previous temples it is much grander in size and scope. It is designed not just for Israel but for all of God's people to gather and celebrate the yearly feasts in Jerusalem. The fact that the millennial temple described here is also equipped to offer sacrifices has caused consternation to many because we believe that Christ is our final sacrifice. First of all, we must remember that not all sacrifices were for atonement of sin. In fact, the majority of offerings brought to the temple in the past were fellowship and thanksgiving offerings to be shared in by those bringing them. Thus bringing sacrifices to the temple especially in the feast days, resulted in a communal barbecue party.

Ezekiel 43:19 does make mention of a sin offering in the final temple. However, it seems best to interpret these sacrifices not as 'expiatory' but rather as 'commemorative,' much like the Lord's supper. As noted before, during the millennium, there will still be sin in the world and these sacrifices may serve as symbolic means of atonement for the penitent. The establishment of the temple with all its rituals further implies that in the millennial kingdom the Lord Jesus will indeed enact the Old Testament legal system as it was originally intended for the nation of Israel. Scriptures are clear that God's Law is perfect (Psalm 19), the problem is human sin and corrupt leaders. So now that Christ is King he will show how God's Law could have and should have been put into practice for the benefit of all mankind.

Chapter 20 of Revelation opens with a strong angel binding the defeated enemy of God, Satan, for 1,000 years. The title of this period, the millennium, takes its name from this number repeated several times in the space of a few verses. While some would like to allegorize or spiritualize this number away, the text is explicit in stating that Christ will rule and reign on earth for 1,000 years. Furthermore, there is really no reason to believe that the text means anything other than what it actually says. To imply otherwise is to call into question God's ability and/or intent to communicate accurately.

The Revelation's brief summary of the millennial reign of Christ focuses on our involvement as co-regents with Christ (Romans 8:17; 2 Timothy 2:12).

> Then I saw thrones, and seated on them were those to whom the authority to judge was committed. Also I saw the souls of those who had been beheaded for the testimony of Jesus and for the word of God, and those who had not worshiped the beast or its image and had not received its mark on their foreheads or their hands. They came to life and reigned with Christ for a thousand years. The rest of the dead did not come to life until the thousand years were ended. This is the first

resurrection. Blessed and holy is the one who shares in the first resurrection! Over such the second death has no power, but they will be priests of God and of Christ, and they will reign with him for a thousand years (Revelation 20:4-6).

Similar to chapter 4, John again sees thrones, but this time they are on the earth. God's purposes have come full circle and now God's heavenly kingdom has once again filled the earth as the waters cover the sea (Habakkuk 2:14). The words from the Lord's Prayer 'your kingdom come' are also finally answered. Jesus' promise that the apostles would sit on thrones and judge the twelve tribes of Israel are likewise fulfilled (Matthew 19:28). The prophets also alluded to a renewed place of authority given to Old Testament saints like David (Ezekiel 34:23-24). Thus, although Christ is the overall King of Kings, others like King David, the apostles and ourselves will be given positions of power and authority in the coming kingdom of Christ on earth. These positions of responsibilities will be given out based on our faithful service to the master in the present age (Matthew 25:14-23).

Next John notices those who have been beheaded for their testimony of Christ during the tribulation. These also will come to life and share in the glories of Christ's kingdom. Initially this may be confusing as the resurrection already took place when all the saints were gathered to Jesus in the clouds just previous to his descent to earth. However, we need to remember that weeks, maybe months transpired between the initial gathering of believers to Christ in the clouds and his actual return to earth. During this time many more presumably trusted in Christ and were subsequently slaughtered by the antichrist and his hordes as they ravaged Jerusalem. Here we find that they are likewise resurrected upon the establishment of Christ's reign, so that no one is left behind. Thus all believers are welcomed to partake in the kingdom of Christ.

Then John speaks to the fate of the rest of the dead, namely those who did not put their trust in Christ. They are not resurrected until the end of the millennium when they will rise from the dead along with all unbelievers from all times to stand before the white throne judgment. This fits in closely with what was revealed to the prophet Daniel (Daniel 12:2). Thus, those who are resurrected at the beginning of the millennium are called blessed as they join Christ in his kingdom, this is the first resurrection (1 Corinthians 15:23). The second death, namely eternal separation from God in the fires of hell, will not be their lot. On the contrary, those that participate in the second resurrection after the millennium, do so for judgment leading to eternal damnation.

Revelation 20 also tells of Satan's final release and his last stand against God and his people. It seems puzzling that even after 1,000 years of peaceful existence under the loving leadership of Christ some would want to join his rebellion. However, we must remember that not everyone who will enter the millennial period will be a believer. Clearly many will choose not to submit whole-heartedly to Jesus and over time this group of disgruntled and ungrateful rebels will only grow. This is further testimony to the utter depravity of man's own heart. So that even in a perfect world, with no demonic temptations or worldly indulgences, the unbelieving heart still proves to be desperately wicked (Jeremiah 17:9).

After the final rebellion is put down, reminiscent of the last battle of armageddon where Gog and Magog played a leading role, the devil is finally dispatched to the place created for him, the fires of hell. Then John sees a great white throne and the Lord seated on it. He notes that at this moment the earth and sky, indeed the whole universe as we know it, will suddenly vanish on account of the glory his presence. The unbelieving dead who are raised up to face judgment are all sentenced to eternal punishment even as death and the grave are also finally done away with. Such will be the end of the world as we know it.

The New Heaven And New Earth

At this time, those that have been redeemed by the Lamb, will finally enter into the full glories of heaven. Revelation 21, gives a breathtaking description of the heavenly Jerusalem which Jesus promised long ago to build for his bride (John 14:1-3). This will be the eternal home of all saints for which they have longed for from time immemorial (Hebrews 11:10, 16). However more amazing than the staggering beauty of this golden city will be the fact that heaven is where God lives among his people forever. Heaven and earth will truly be united in complete harmony.

Some interesting features of this eternal state stand out to John, namely the absence of a sea. The reason is not stated but it may be because the sea was often used to represent the dark forces of evil, which will now be extinct. He also notes that there is no need for the sun, moon and stars because the light of God's glory will more than suffice to illuminate heaven. Most importantly, John notes the absence of the curse, namely suffering, sin and death will be completely eradicated. What a joy it will be to live in a world where evil can no longer find a foothold.

John also spends some time detailing some of the surprising elements of heaven. First is the fact that heaven is a glorious city decked out like a bride on her wedding day, this in contrast to the lewd capital city of the antichrist, Babylon the Great. The reference to a bride here is not to be confused with Paul's metaphorical designation of the church as Christ's wife in Ephesians 5. What John describes in stunning detail is in fact a real city and our eternal home.

And he carried me away in the Spirit to a great, high mountain, and showed me the holy city Jerusalem coming down out of heaven from God, having the glory of God, its radiance like a most rare jewel, like a jasper, clear as crystal. It had a great, high wall, with twelve gates, and at the gates twelve angels, and on the gates the names of the twelve tribes of the sons of Israel were inscribed— on the east three gates, on the north three gates, on the south three gates, and on the west three gates. And the wall of the city had twelve foundations, and on them were the twelve names of the twelve apostles of the Lamb. And the one who spoke with me had a measuring rod of gold to measure the city and its gates and walls. The city lies foursquare, its length the same as its width. And he measured the city with his rod, 12,000 stadia. Its length and width and height are equal. He also measured its wall, 144 cubits by human measurement, which is also an angel's measurement. The wall was built of jasper, while the city was pure gold, like clear glass. The foundations of the wall of the city were adorned with every kind of jewel. The first was jasper, the second sapphire, the third agate, the fourth emerald, the fifth onyx, the sixth carnelian, the seventh chrysolite, the eighth beryl, the ninth topaz, the tenth chrysoprase, the eleventh jacinth, the twelfth amethyst. And the twelve gates were twelve pearls, each of the gates made of a single pearl, and the street of the city was pure gold, like transparent glass. And I saw no temple in the city, for its temple is the Lord God the Almighty and the Lamb (Revelation 21:10-22).

Any attempt to interpret the above description of the New Jerusalem as anything less than what it literally says does a great injustice to God's Word. How could we allegorize the specific measurements provided by the apostle John? This was not the fruit of an excited imagination but rather of empirical investigation. The fact that the city displays the names of both the twelve tribes and the twelve apostles, again serves to underscore that God's final plan for mankind is not one where we are all divided up according to our ethnic or denominational heritage, but rather one where we will all melded together into one great family united under the banner of Christ. As to the residents of this glorious metropolis the letter of Hebrews gives us some more details:

But you have come to Mount Zion and to the city of the living God, the heavenly Jerusalem, and to innumerable angels in festal gathering, and to the assembly of the firstborn who are enrolled in heaven, and to God, the judge of all, and to the spirits of the righteous made perfect, and to Jesus, the mediator of a new covenant, and to the sprinkled blood that speaks a better word than the blood of Abel (Hebrews 12:22-24).

Before wrapping up his description of the heavenly city, John also notes some other surprising elements therein. He makes a note of the river of life and the tree of life in the middle of the New Jerusalem. These final fixtures take us right back to the beginning of creation, to the Garden of Eden, when these were lost to mankind on account of our rebellion. Indeed the eternal state will be a grand composite of both the original and the redeemed. It will be a glorious garden within a city in which all the saints live in ethereal peace and perfect harmony. Most significantly, John notes that we will all 'see his face.' Indeed all the joys of heaven will be eclipsed by the sheer joy of gazing on the face of our great God and Savior. *"As for me, I shall behold your face in righteousness; when I awake, I shall be satisfied with your likeness"* (Psalm 17:15).

Thus the Revelation comes to a glorious conclusion with the Lord Jesus promising to come soon with reward in hand and reminding his followers three times to remain watchful: *"Behold I come quickly!"*

Conclusion

In our brief road trip through the Revelation we have surely missed some scenic points or historic details. However, regardless of our years of spiritual maturity, I hope we have all seen some new vistas along the way. I sure have! Most importantly I trust we can appreciate the larger picture better. Also, like any good journey, such an experience should always leave us wanting to travel down those familiar lanes again looking for new sights, always wanting to glean a deeper appreciation of the landscape. As your guide in this tour, if I have succeeded in anything, I hope it is in whetting your appetite to revisit the Revelation with greater gusto again and again. Likewise, I hope it has given you cause to believe that this 'graveyard of interpreters' can indeed come to life like Ezekiel's valley of bones.

Hopefully you have seen that the Revelation is not as unintelligible as many imagine it to be. However if we approach it with sloppy hermeneutical skills and skewed theological frameworks we will surely find ourselves frustrated. On the other hand if we let the Biblical text lead the way soon we will find that the picture comes into focus beautifully. Indeed, as the time of the end appears, we can expect to begin seeing the eschatological puzzle take shape before our eyes. As we enter those troubled waters ahead let's be sure to have our Biblical compass and eschatological map handy and ready to go.

We've noted in this chapter that the book of Revelation outlines itself quite beautifully in 1:19. Accordingly, starting in chapter 4, the Revelation turns its attention to events yet future. The seven sealed scroll that the Lord Jesus opens turns out to be God's indictment of mankind. The seven seals further serve as an outline of the seven year tribulation, starting with the antichrist's promises of peace and ending in the chaos of armageddon.

The text largely focuses on the final couple of years and months of the tribulation when God's judgments will be poured out on mankind. At that time, the Lord Jesus will suddenly appear and gather all saints, dead or alive, to join him in the clouds. Then in the sky, in plain sight of all the world, he will be given dominion and proclaimed the Royal Priest even as the heavenly temple is opened. At that time the 'judgment seat of Christ' and 'marriage supper of the Lamb' will also take place.

Even as the Lord sets up his temporary headquarters in the clouds, the antichrist will be gathering all his forces against

Israel hoping to obliterate God's people and bring to naught his promises. During this time he will fight against the two witnesses and 144,000 Jewish believers ultimately killing them. However when the exiled and embattled nation of Israel finally repents and begin to mourn over the loss of her Messiah, Christ will begin his victorious procession to earth. Starting in the wilderness Christ will gather his scattered people as he makes his way to Jerusalem. Finally, his feet will land on the Mount of Olives and he will completely vanquish the antichrist and his hordes with the sword of judgment emanating from his mouth.

Then Christ will sit on the throne of David and begin his millennial reign on earth. He will judge all the inhabitants of the earth even as those martyred in the final phase of the tribulation come back to life to join him in his reign. Thus Jesus will be the King of the World, ruling from his new capital city Jerusalem. Peace and prosperity will ensue, but after 1,000 years there will still be those who refuse to wholeheartedly submit to him. After defeating their final rebellion led by Satan, Christ will abolish the universe as we know it. Unbelievers will be judged and condemned to an eternity without God. Believers on the other hand will be welcomed into the new heaven and the new earth where they will dwell forever in God's presence.

OUR RESPONSE

opefully by now you are feeling some real excitement and anticipation about the glorious future mapped out for us in the Bible. However, I'm sure this is also tempered with more than a little apprehension as to the challenging days ahead. My hope is that you have at least become convinced of the urgent nature of this subject. All the pieces of the eschatological puzzle may not be sitting quite well with you yet but be assured that as you faithfully pursue the Lord and scour his Word the picture will become clearer. This is, until one day, it is no longer just a picture anymore, but the real face of our Savior Jesus Christ standing before us in all his majesty. As the words of the old hymn remind us:

> *It will be worth it all*
> *when we see Jesus!*
> *Life's trials will seem so small*
> *when we see Christ.*
> *One glimpse of his dear face,*
> *all sorrow will erase.*
> *So, bravely run the race*
> *till we see Christ.[49]*

Speaking of this one moment, the greatest moment of our existence, C.S. Lewis writes, "*In the end that Face which is the delight or the terror of the universe must be turned upon each of us either with one expression or with the other, either conferring glory inexpressible or inflicting shame that can never be cured or disguised."* In preparation for that momentous occasion our heart's unabashed longing should be to hear the 'divine accolade': WELL DONE! This is why we were created, this is what we lived for, to hear and know that our heavenly Father is truly pleased with us. Lewis summarizes it beautifully,

> *"To please God...to be a real ingredient in the divine happiness...to be loved by God, not merely pitied, but delighted in as an artist delights in his work or a father in his son - it seems impossible, a weight or burden of glory which our thoughts can hardly sustain. But so it is."*[50]

In the meantime what do we do with this tremendous burden of revelation ? How do we go on living normal lives? I think that is just it, we must recognize we are not called to be normal and should not seek to live merely normal lives. We need to rise above the mundane and allow the knowledge of Christ's return and kingdom to energize us day in and day out as it did the believers in the first century (2 Timothy 4:1-5). As noted earlier our eschatological studies should never be disconnected from our practical Christian lives, rather they should help mold us more into the image of Christ and motivate us to greater service for him.

In the many passages that touch on the end times, the authors of Scriptures often take a moment to call us to appropriate action in light of eschatological truths. Their injunctions are summarized below and can serve as a regular checkup list for us as we draw ever nearer to the most challenging and exciting time of human history.

1. Stay awake and alert!
   a. *"So also, when you see all these things, you know that He is near, at the very gates"* (Matthew 24:33).
   b. *"Be on guard, keep awake. For you do not know when the time will come"* (Mark 13:33).
   c. *"So then let us not sleep, as others do, but let us keep awake and be sober"* (1 Thessalonians 5:6).

      d. *"Behold, I am coming like a thief! Blessed is the one who stays awake, keeping his garments on, that he may not go about naked and be seen exposed!"* (Revelation 16:15).

2. Heed the warnings!

      a. Deception: False Prophets/Teaching (Luke 17:22-34; 21:8-36)

            i. Do not go after them! (Luke 21:8)

            ii. Do not believe them! (Matthew 24:23-26)

            iii. Do not be shaken! (2 Thessalonians 2:3; 1 Timothy 4:1-2)

      b. Disasters: Wars, revolts, plagues, earthquakes, famines ... (Matthew 24)

            i. Do not be terrified (Luke 21:9)

            ii. Do not be surprised! (Matthew 24:6-8)

            iii. Do not grow faint! (Luke 21:25-28)

      c. Distress: Great Persecution and Martyrdom (Daniel 12:1; Revelation 6:9)

            i. Do not be anxious! (Matthew 24:9-11)

            ii. Do not give in! (Matthew 24:12-13; Luke 21:19)

            iii. Do not miss the opportunity! (Matthew 24:14; Luke 21:13)

      d. Depravity: Immorality/Complacency

            i. Do not get caught up in it! (Luke 17:26-33, 2 Timothy 3:1-5)

            ii. Do not get weighted down! (Luke 21:34-36; 2 Peter 3:10-13)

            iii. Do not be caught off guard! (Romans 13:11-14; 1 Thessalonians 5:3-8)

3. Invest in God's Kingdom!

      a. *"Do not lay up for yourselves treasures on earth, where moth and rust destroy and where thieves break in and steal, but lay up for yourselves treasures in heaven, where neither moth nor rust* destroys and where thieves do not break in and steal. For where your treasure is, there your heart will be also" (Matthew 6:19-21).

b. "His master said to him, Well done, good and faithful servant. You have been faithful over a little; I will set you over much. Enter into the joy of your master" (Matthew 25:21)

c. "But as it is, they desire a better country, that is, a heavenly one. Therefore God is not ashamed to be called their God, for he has prepared for them a city" (Hebrews 11:16).

4. Be busy in God's business!

a. "Therefore, stay awake, for you do not know on what day your Lord is coming" (Matthew 24:42).

b. "Blessed is that servant whom his master will find so doing when he comes" (Matthew 24:46).

c. "I charge you in the presence of God and of Christ Jesus, who is to judge the living and the dead, and by his appearing and his kingdom: preach the word; be ready in season and out of season; reprove, rebuke, and exhort, with complete patience and teaching" (2 Timothy 4:1-2).

5. Shine like the Sun!

a. "And those who are wise (have insight) shall shine like the brightness of the sky above; and those who turn many to righteousness, like the stars forever and ever" (Daniel 12:3).

b. "Walk in wisdom toward outsiders, making the best use of the time. Let your speech always be gracious, seasoned with salt, so that you may know how you ought to answer each person" (Colossians 4:5-6).

6. Seize the Day!

a. "Many shall purify themselves and make themselves white and be refined, but the wicked shall act wickedly. And none of the wicked shall understand, but those who are wise shall understand" (Daniel 12:10).

b. *"Look carefully then how you walk, not as unwise but as wise, making the best use of the time, because the days are evil"* (Ephesians 5:15-16).

7. Hold on to the promises!

a. *"Let us hold fast the confession of our hope without wavering, for he who promised is faithful. And let us consider how to stir up one another to love and good works, not neglecting to meet together, as is the habit of some, but encouraging one another, and all the more as you see the Day drawing near"* (Hebrews 10:23-25).

b. *"Now to him who is able to keep you from stumbling and to present you blameless before the presence of his glory with great joy, to the only God, our Savior, through Jesus Christ our Lord, be glory, majesty, dominion, and authority, before all time and now and forever. Amen"* (Jude 24-25).

Finally our ultimate goal should always be to remain pure and holy as we await our glorious bridegroom (2 Corinthians 11:2). This involves striving for both personal integrity and harmonious relationships with those around us, especially those who have a different take on eschatology! *"Strive for peace with everyone, and for the holiness without which no one will see the Lord"* (Hebrews 12:14). We do this so that when the day finally comes that we stand before our Lord and Savior, we can truly bask unashamed in the glory of his presence (1 Thessalonians 2:19; 1 John 2:28).

Now may the God of peace himself sanctify you completely, and may your whole spirit and soul and body be kept blameless at the coming of our Lord Jesus Christ. He who calls you is faithful; he will surely do it (1 Thessalonians 5:23-24).

END NOTES

[1] Tim LaHaye, Jerry Jenkins, *Are we living in the End Times*, (Tyndale, 2011) pg. 3

[2] Chuck Missler, *Cosmic Codes*, (Koinonia House, 1999) pg. 47.

[3] This fact is further attested to by empirical science in the *anthropic* principle, otherwise known as the fine-tuning argument.

[4] Quran 2:34; 7:11.

[5] Flavius Josephus, *The Antiquities of the Jews* (Book 1, Chapter 4).

[6] Tim Lahaye, Ed Hindson, *The Popular Bible Prophecy Commentary.* (Harvest House, 2006) pg. 23.

[7] Ronald Diprose, *Israel and the church* (Authentic Media, 2000) pg. 168

[8] While this secondary meaning is challenged by some, Greek lexicons like BAGD confirm it.

[9] This actually fulfills the longing of Moses in which he wished all believers were filled with the Holy Spirit (Numbers 11:29).

[10] It is important for us Gentile believers to be sensitive to our Jewish brothers and sisters who may chose to still abide by the Law's regulations. In this regard, our repeated references to the 'Old' Covenant, can be offensive to them. Indeed, most believers would agree that although we may not be bound to the ceremonial laws of the Law we still recognize the universal value of the moral code enshrined therein. Thus, it might be best to refer to it as the 'first' or 'original' covenant.

[11] Examples of this truth are evident in the Bible as men like Job and Melchizedek, both Gentiles, clearly attained a deep and personal relationship with God outside of Israel.

[12] Interestingly, to this day, Psalm 118 is read by Jewish people in their Passover celebrations.

[13] Paul Benware, *Understanding End Times Prophecy.* (Moody, 1995) pg. 26-27.

[14] Walvoord and Zuck. *The Bible Knowledge Commentary: Old Testament.* (Victor Books, 1985) pg 1361.

[15] This misinterpretation has further been hampered by mistranslations like that of the usually trustworthy NASB, which do not follow the Hebrew text sentence structure and instead link the 7 and 62 weeks.

[16] I should also note that I am aware of the usual attempts to harmonize these verses with Jewish history, including Sir Robert Anderson's intriguing work. However, later research has found issues with such interpretations. Thus it seems best to interpret this passage in a straight-forward manner giving attention to the historic context rather than forcing it to fit into a New Testament timeline.

[17] Josephs, Antiquities of the Jews (Book XI, Chapter 5.7)

[18] Some are surprised to hear that Jesus was not born on year one. The fact is that the monks of the Middle Ages who set up our current calendar didn't get it quite right. This is further evidenced by the fact that Herod the Great, who tried to kill baby Jesus, died in 4 B.C. which pushes the birth of Jesus back to 5-6 B.C.

[19] Regarding the interpretation I've outlined for the first two segments of the 70 Week Prophecy I should note that I am partially indebted to Fred Zaspel's article "Daniel's 'Seventy Weeks': A Historical and Exegetical Analysis (1991). Online: http://www.biblicalstudies.com/bstudy/eschatology/daniel.htm (this link appears to be no longer operative).

[20] For a detailed analysis of this important historical fact see: www.hope-of-israel.org/peopleofprince.html

[21] The Hebrew verb used here Shamem is usually translated as 'causes desolation'. However it can also mean 'to stun or cause amazement'. Revelation 13 tells of how the nations will be amazed at the antichrist's miraculous power causing them to worship him. This in particular with regard to some kind of speaking statue that the false prophet sets up for the former. Thus the 'abomination' may in fact be a pagan statue much like the one erected in the Jewish temple by Antiochus in 167 B.C.

[22] Paul Maier, Eusebius The Church History. (Kregel, 2007) pg. 82-90.

[23] John Walvoord, The Revelation of Jesus Christ (Moody 1989) pg. 197.

[24] Much speculation has been made about the 'red' coloring of the beast. However it likely speaks to the blood of the saints which he wantonly spills.

[25] Joel Richardson, Mystery Babylon (WND Books, 2017).

[26] The fact that each head represents both a kingdom and its leading king or most prominent king is exemplified by similar usage in Daniel 7.

[27] This is why to this day, the Greek Orthodox in Turkey are called 'Rum' i.e. Romans.

[28] Philip Jenkins, *The Lost History of Christianity* (Harper One, 2008) pg. 148-49

[29] Jason Goodwin, *Lords of the Horizon* (Owl Books, 1998) pg. 8

[30] R.Laird Harris, Gleason Archer and Bruce Waltke, *Theological Wordbook of the Old Testament* Vol II (Moody, 1980) pg. 825

[31] Geoffrey Bromiley, *The International Standard Bible Encyclopedia* Vol. II (Eerdmans, 1982) pg. 524

[32] Geoffrey Bromiley, *The International Standard Bible Encyclopedia* Vol. III (Eerdmans, 1982) pg. 328

[33] Ibid. pg. 222

[34] Tim Lahaye, Ed Hindson, *The Popular Bible Prophecy Commentary.* (Harvest House, 2006) pg. 191.

[35] Some early church fathers like Tertullian held this view, namely that civil law and order had a restraining effect on Satan's ambitions to completely destroy humanity.

[36] Tim Lahaye, Ed Hindson, *The Popular Bible Prophecy Commentary.* (Harvest House, 2006) pg. 455

[37] This view is expounded in detail by Colin Nicholl. Online: www.jstor.org/stable/pdf/23967739.pdf

[38] Joel Richardson in his seminal book *Mideast Beast,* goes into much more detail on this intriguing correlation.

[39] David Bercot, *A Dictionary of Early Christian Beliefs* (Hendrickson, 1998) pg. 551.

[40] Wayne Grudem, *Systematic Theology* (IVP, 1994) pg. 1100.

[41] Mal Couch, *Dictionary of Premillennial Theology* (Kregel, 1996) pg 43-44.

[42] John MacArthur, *The MacArthur New Testament Commentary: Revelation 1-11* (Moody, 1999) pg 20-21.

[43] It is important to make the connection here with Daniel 7:9-10, in which God is likewise seen seated on the throne, ready to judge the nations even as the books are opened.

[44] Robert Thomas, An Exegetical Commentary: Revelation 1-7 (Moody, 1992) pg. 375-379.

[45] Hebrews 8:5 explicitly notes that all earthly temples were tailored after the original heavenly sanctuary. At Christ's second coming this perfect sanctuary will be made visible for all the world to see.

[46] The Greek word used here for mark, charagma, was usually used of a visible mark like a tattoo or seal that was designed to identify something as belonging to someone. Thus, slaves and soldiers were

often tattooed with the names of their owners or regiment. In this way such a mark really represented a pledge of allegiance.

[47] Ancient languages gave numerical values to letters so that everyone's name had a numerical equivalent that served as their 'Identification Number.'

[48] Robert Thomas, An Exegetical Commentary: Revelation 8-22. (Moody, 1995) pg. 268-269

[49] Written by Esther Kerr Rusthoi

[50] Taken from C.S. Lewis' sermon titled "The Weight of Glory" preached in the Church of St Mary the Virgin, Oxford, on June 8, 1942.

ABOUT THE AUTHOR

Jerry Mattix

Jerry Mattix and his wife Sarah serve as ambassadors of Jesus Christ in the Middle East. Jerry, born to Christian missionary parents in Bolivia, has dedicated his life to the service of God and people in need of the gospel. He has authored numerous Christian books in English but also in Turkish under the pen name Can Nuroğlu. Sarah is a trauma counselor. Together they are raising their three children and continue serving their Lord and Savior Jesus Christ in Northern Cyprus.

BOOKS BY THIS AUTHOR

Jesus Alone

Jesus Christ is undoubtedly the most influential and inspiring person in history. And yet today most know his name only as a byword. The true Jesus of the Bible has become shrouded in layers of mystical and religious paraphernalia. It is time to unveil his true character and appreciate him in light of his historical context.

In this book Jerry Mattix seeks to take us back to the heart of Christianity, to meet the person of Jesus Christ. Just like his first followers sought to express in writing the amazing truths they witnessed to their generation, the author hopes to take those same historical facts and make them understandable to this generation.

Dear Muslim Friend

Dear Muslim Friend seeks to answer the basic questions Muslims are commonly asking about Christianity. These include: Hasn't the Bible been changed? How could Isa [Jesus] be the Son of God? Didn't someone else die on the cross instead of Isa [Jesus]? Misunderstanding on these and related issues continues to feed the misconception that cloud East and West relations. This book is designed to provide answers in an easily-understood format. More importantly, it sheds light on God's truth as it relates to the salvation God offers to all people.

Dear Skeptic Friend

Dear Skeptic Friend strives to present logical answers to the big questions of life based both on the biblical narrative and verifiable scientific data–questions like:

Can belief in God stand the test of logic and science?

If God exists, how can he allow so much evil in the world?

How can we possibly trust the Bible to be reliable?

What about all the contradictions in the scriptures?

Humans are wired to inquire. People long to find answers to life's most essential enigmas. Tackling these tough issues is not only reasonable, but also necessary if we hope to have any peace of mind.

Democracy In The Middle East

Tragic developments in the Middle East remind us again and again of the utter failure of Western states to establish democracy in Muslim majority countries. Since the outset of the 'war on terror', the investment of trillions of dollars in this troubled region, aiming to foment and foster liberal values, have only resulted in creating a quagmire of diplomatic gridlock and political bankruptcy. The question still looms large: Why has democracy failed so miserably in the Middle East?

This book is an unabridged reproduction of a thesis which was completed in 2016 for the Eastern Mediterranean University Political Science Department in fulfillment of a Master's degree in International Relations, yet its content is as relevant today as ever. The author, Jerry Mattix, who has lived in the Middle East for over 20 years, interviewed a representative sample of 16 students from across the Middle East asking them critical questions related to democracy. Their answers paint a stark picture of the failure of democracy in the Middle East but also help to highlight the changes that need to be made.

Made in the USA
Middletown, DE
05 August 2022